To Geoff,

ROSELAWN 2021

Thanks, for your support.

GW00702808

Peter McCabe

Roselawn 2021

Self-published

pmtours27@gmail.com
07596 603463

Contents

Foreword

I first met Peter in April 2017 as we were planning our Talks & Tours programme ahead of our annual EastSide Arts Festival. Peter was 'pitching' a guided tour of Belfast City Cemetery and had sent through a whole list of names of significant individuals and families from east Belfast who were buried in the west of the city. A trend which has continued to this day.

I must confess, I was a little sceptical about the appeal of such a tour however agreed to meet Peter at the gates of the cemetery for a preview. This was my first visit to Belfast City Cemetery and I was genuinely enthralled as Peter led us through these peaceful grounds and brought a range of graves to life through fascinating stories and quirky anecdotes.

Peter's uniquely relaxed and 'at ease' personality shone through as he served up a mix of humour and poignancy, conjuring up emotions which I had previously thought were contradictory. However, when combined through Peter's naturally respectful style, these can in fact be very much complementary of each other.

It has been quite a journey with Peter since that first Spring afternoon with his sell-out guided tours becoming a staple of EastSide Partnership's arts and heritage activity throughout the year. Peter was one of our first locals to sign up to our voluntary 'EastSide Greeter' scheme and is also now a Greenway Leader proudly championing the responsible use of our much-loved Connswater Community Greenway.

Peter often describes himself as 'your local taphophile' but to me he is much more than that. In my mind, Peter is a natural storyteller who expertly connect groups, audiences and readers with extraordinary subjects from the past – people who often made a real difference when they were living. Now, thanks to Peter and his diligent, unrelenting research, stories of these local pioneers and their achievements live on and continue to make a positive impact on our lives today.

I had the pleasure of joining Peter's first official guided walking tour of Roselawn Cemetery back in August 2020 and so I can certainly vouch for some incredible stories of achievement, triumph, conflict, loss, resilience, pride, love and of course good humour.

I very much hope you enjoy this book and I would personally like to thank Peter for bringing these enriching stories back to life.

Chris Armstrong
EastSide Partnership

Introduction

After mediocre success with books about Belfast City Cemetery, Dundonald Cemetery, and then '2020' (20 graves in each of 20 selected local cemeteries), and with a book called 'Hundred Houses of East Belfast' in the pipeline, I decided to spend a fair chunk of lockdown writing another book about a cemetery. The cemetery this time is Roselawn, with this publication called '2021'.

Until fairly recently, I had only a passing interest in Roselawn (with the exception of the grave of my much-missed maternal grandparents whose wedding photograph features on the front cover, with an image of their headstone on the back cover of this publication) due to the relative 'newness' of the cemetery which only opened in 1954.

However, whilst researching my 'Hundred Houses of East Belfast' book, I discovered that, amongst the thousands of graves there, not forgetting the thousands of memorial trees in Roselawn too, there are many fascinating headstones with, I think, associated fascinating stories.

So my daily lockdown exercise when Roselawn was open – obviously, although it wouldn't be the first time I've climbed over a fence to get in and out of a cemetery – consisted of walking round every headstone in the cemetery, photographing headstones of interest and then looking into the story behind each for the purposes of a book.

So, after wearing down the soles of my shoes, I've come up with 'Roselawn 2021', consisting of 20 themed trails, each calling at 21 headstones.

The 21 graves in each themed trail are in date order of the main person featured at each plot, and I have enclosed a number of photos to accompany the text in each of the 20 trails.

I am, of course, available to lead tours around Roselawn so, if you belong to a group who might be interested in a bespoke wander round Roselawn, or even if a few of your family and friends would be interested, please get in touch using the contact details on page 2.

I'm also available for presentations about Roselawn, or any of the other cemeteries covered in previous books, so again, if this would be of interest, I'd be keen to hear from you.

As with previous books this has been a team effort, so my thanks go to Nigel Henderson for all his help assisting me to find further information on so many of the entries, and thanks to Eddie Connolly for his help with this too.

Thanks also to Clive Scoular for proof-reading this publication, and to Chris Armstrong from EastSide Partnership for writing the foreword and for his support with my two sold-out tours of Roselawn during the EastSide Arts Festival of 2020 and 2021.

Sincere thanks to everyone who has donated towards this project, especially James Brown of James Brown & Sons, John Costley, Andrew Wylie and Stewart McCracken. I'm also grateful to everyone who sponsored a trail, some even doing so willingly, without me having to twist their arms.

Finally, big love and thanks to my Mum and Dad for continuing to indulge me in this mid-life crisis whilst, like the previous tomes, this publication is dedicated to Jana who continues to inspire.

Peter, December 2021

Trail 1 – Quirky

Trail 1 is sponsored by Andrew Wylie, a Belfast boy now living in Northamptonshire.

This first trail features, with respect, unusual quirky commemorations, including Billy Fonda an Elvis impersonator, the 'Bard of Ballynafeigh' and the 'Kebab Man'.

William James (Willie) Mitchell - D-1110 - this headstone states that Mitchell 'died 21st March 1960, aged 62 years (of heart failure, not by drowning) in Victoria Park, Sydenham'. Mitchell was living at 31 Nevis Avenue, Belfast when he died, with the base of the headstone stating 'On Christ the solid rock I stand all other grounds are sinking sands', and 'Nobly you fought your knightly virtue proved. Your memory hallowed in the land you loved. Is[aiah].53:9 (16-21)'. This headstone also commemorates that Mitchell was 'second son of the late George and Charlotte Anne Mitchell (Interred Dundonald)' Cemetery, Plot E2-126.

William Montgomery - C-26 - 'Born 1881 - Died 1965. Cast a cold Eye On life, on Death. Horseman, pass by', the same epitaph that William Butler Yeats wrote for himself, and engraved on his headstone in the churchyard of Drumcliff, county Sligo. William was living at 98 Boundary Street, Belfast when he died on 11 February 1965 aged 83. Also buried in this grave is Stephen Montgomery, 'Born 1926 - Died 1982. He fought the good fight. He finished his course. He kept the faith'. Stephen was living at 20 Innisfayle Gardens, Belfast when be died on 7 August 1982 aged 56. Also commemorated on this headstone is  Rachel Hegarty 'Born 1959 - Died 2006. God has found another angel', who was living at 292c Shore Crescent, Belfast when she died on 31 January 2006 aged 46.

William D Dwyer - T-2004 - this headstone was erected 'in loving memory of William Down (Billy) darling husband of (space) died 26th November 1972' aged 57 whilst registered as living at 30 Merok Crescent, Belfast. There is a space between the words 'of' and 'died', where it appears that a word has been foricbly removed from the headstone! The burial records show that Jean Dwyer, who was also living at 30 Merok Crescent when she died on 28 April 1998 aged 68, is also buried in this plot, but is not commemorated on the headstone, or anywhere at this

plot. Jean was aged 42 when William died aged 57 in 1972, so I wonder if there was perhaps a family fall-out in the time between their respective deaths, which has lead to the wording on the headstone being changed?

Richard Finlay - T-3840 - '1906 - 1974. Devoted husband and father' Finlay was registered as living at 192 Shore Road, Newtownabbey when he died on 28 March 1974 aged 68, with the base of this headstone reading 'But thy eternal summer shall not fade. Shakespeare', a quote from the Bard's 'Shall I compare thee to a summer's day?' (Sonnet 18).

George Ernest Stears - V-1028 - commemorated on the headstone as a 'Pioneer Missionary to Brasilian Indians', Stears was living at 34b Forthriver Crescent, Belfast when he died on 3 July 1980 aged 82. Also remembered on this headstone is 'his beloved wife Lilian Stears died 27th October 1983 aged 85 years', whilst a resident of Clifton House, Belfast.

Fullalove - R-1248 - this headstone, with the unusual name of Fullalove at the top, was erected 'in loving memory of our dear grandparents Edward died 29th December 1985' aged 77 whilst living at Fold 30, 37 Fortwilliam Park, Belfast, and 'Veronica died 21st May 1992' aged 82 whilst living at 32 Cranmore Avenue, Belfast. Also commemorated on this headstone is 'their beloved daughter our devoted mother Elizabeth [who] died 24th June 2019' with the words 'Rest In Peace' at the base of the headstone. Interestingly there are other Fullalove headstones in Roselawn. Plot S-3098 contains the remains of Elizabeth Fullalove who died on 6 October 1992 aged 58, Jane Fullalove who died on 22 March 1982, and Paul Fullalove who died on 22 January 1995 aged 70, all three dying whilst registered as living at 9 Circular Road, Belfast.

Joan Patricia Bramston - R-3136 - this headstone remembers 'Joan Patricia who fell asleep 21st November 1992 Beloved wife of Reginald who fell asleep 7th January 1997 who rests here with her 'date''. Joan was living at 31 Belmont Church Road, Belfast when she died aged 63, whilst her 'date' Reginald died at Kirk House, Kings Road, Belfast aged 79. The base of this headstone reads 'In faith we will rise together'.

John (Jackie) McCracken - P-1802 - 'Born 15th August 1955 Boldly went to the final frontier 12th January 1997 aged 42 years. Beloved husband, father, son and brother', with the base of this headstone reading 'The eternal God is your refuge and dwelling place and underneath thy everlasting arms, Deuteronomy 33.27'. I think there's a fair chance that Jackie - who was living at 21 Abbot Gardens, Newtownards when he died - was a big Star Trek fan.

William Thomas Johnston - S-68 - 'Died 20th December 1998. He was an adored friend to Nat, Barbara and Angela. A musician, an Elvis impressionist (Billy Fonda) Bill grew up on Donegall Rd, The Village, Belfast. Laid to 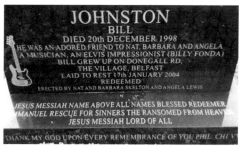 rest 17th December 2004 Redeemed. Erected by Nat and Barbara Skelton and Angela Lewis'. Bill was registered as living at 61 Donegall Avenue, Belfast when he died aged 57. The base of this headstone states 'Jesus Messiah name above all names, Blessed redeemer Emmanuel, Rescue for sinners the ransomed from heaven, Jesus Messiah Lord of all. I thank my God upon every remembrance of you. Phil. Ch1 v3'. Another Elvis fan, Robert Parker, is buried at R-1965. 'A beloved husband and father ... 25-12-1943 - 19-1-1988' aged 44, Parker was living at 41 Kilbroney Bend, Belfast when he died, with an Elvis signature at the top of this headstone.

Robert Christopher (Roy) Gildea - D-2300 - the top of this headstone states 'Ship Ahoy Roy'. Gildea, '7-6-51 16-11-99', was living at 14 Maymount Street, Belfast when he died aged 48. Also buried in this grave is 'Frances Margaret Rose [Gildea] 19-6-18 7-7-2011' who died aged 63 whilst also living at 14 Maymount Street. Along with a number of symbols including a ship, anchor and butterfly, this headstone states 'We are in astral plains dancing together again'.

Isabella Duff - R-4039 - this headstone commemorates 'Hugh Mallinson Duff Born 22nd March 1926 Died 18th August 1992, whilst registered as living at 5 Knockvale Park, Belfast. The headstone contains the logos for the Merchant Navy and GCHQ (Government Communications Headquarters). Also commemorated on the headstone is 'his beloved wife Isabella (nee Curry) 26th Nov 1929 - 3rd Aug 2017 Mother Grandmother and Great-Grandmother'. Amusingly the inscription then states 'This is the quietest she has ever been', with the base of the headstone then stating 'Loved by all'.

Mary Doyle - W-904 - 'A beloved wife, mother and grandmother Mary died 28th September 2006. For compared with her, all gold is a pinch of sand'. Doyle was living at 62 Rushfield Avenue, Belfast when she died aged 60, with the base of the headstone stating 'Forever Thirty Nine'. Also buried in this plot is 'her husband Tommy a devoted family man Died 11th January 2018 "The Bard of Ballynafeigh"'. The Bard of Ballynafeigh seems to have been a self-appointed position of Doyle's.

John Patrick Donnelly - W-999 - 'Died 1st October 2007 aged 60 years "Programme Completed, I will rest in peace"'. Donnelly was living at Rosemount House, 424 Antrim Road, Belfast at the time of his death. The use of the term 'programme completed' would suggest that Donnelly was either a computer programmer or, and perhaps more likely, as the term is apparently used in this context, signifying that he had completed an Alcoholics Anonymous programme successfully.

John Lawrence Robertson - W-1055 - 'A much loved husband, father and brother 12th December 1934 – 5th November 2008' aged 73, Robertson died whilst living at 80 Alexandra Park Avenue, Belfast. A miniature of Robertson malt scotch whisky, containing the Robertson clan crest, sits at the base of this headstone, with the top of the headstone also featuring the Robertson crest, a dexter hand holding up an imperial crown with the motto 'Virtutis Gloria Merces' (Glory is the reward of valour).

Malcolm (Red) McCalmont - W-2893 - 'in loving memory of a devoted husband father grandfather and great-grandfather passed away 12th April 2014'. At the top of the headstone, either side of the inscription, is a purple beret suggesting that McCalmont perhaps served with the Parachute Regiment, along with the representation of a pint of Tennents. Also commemorated on the headstone is 'his beloved wife Anna Elizabeth (Lily) a much loved mother, grandmother and great-grandmother passed away 9th November 2018'. A plaque at the base of the headstone states 'We hold you close within our hearts and there you shall remain to walk with us through our lives until we meet again'.

Robert (Bobby) Smyth - W-2891 - 'in loving memory of [a] beloved husband, dad and grandad Born 19.09.42 Called home 23.08.14'. The base of this headstone states 'Be still, and know that I am God', whilst a plaque at the bottom of the grave reads 'Peace I leave with you, my peace I give unto you, not as the world giveth give I unto you, let not your heart be troubled, neither let it be afraid John Ch.14.v27', with the representation of a steak van commemorating 'Bobby, the steak burger grill' beside the headstone.

Elmekki Berrabah - W-4017 - '"Kebab Man" Returned To Allah On 12th April 2015' with the base of the headstone stating 'Forever in our hearts'. The 'Kebab Man' is buried in a small Muslim section of the cemetery, with the section screened off from the neighbouring section by a large hedge. When compiling an article on the cemetery prior to a couple of tours that I led as part of 2020's EastSide Arts Festival, Ivan Little was able to establish that, rather than working at the Sphinx on the Stranmillis Road in Belfast as I had thought, Berrabah was actually living and working in Campsie when he died.

Sheila Roberts Carson - S-2712 - this rectangular smooth slab of stone commemorates Carson 'nee Deane 1929 - 2016. The mountains are calling and I must go...', with a number of stones at the base of the headstone. Also buried in this grave is 'Martha Jane Deane 1904 - 1984' who died on 3 July 1984 aged 79, whilst registered as living at 33 Orangefield Crescent, Belfast.

Ramzan Bibi - W-4027 - 'in the name of Allah most gracious, most merciful in memory of Ramzan Bibi wife of Mohammad Yaseen Dean will never be forgotten by her sons; Amin, Saleem and Arif By daughter; Shazia and Grandsons; Talha and Daaniyaal. Returned to Allah 14th May 2016. "Remember O man as you pass by, as you are now so once was I, As I am now so you must be, Prepare O man to follow me"'. This grave is again in a small Muslim section of the cemetery, and I feel it merits inclusion in the Quirky section as the unusual verse at the bottom of the headstone is more regularly found on Christian graves.

Eddie Doyle - W-902 - 'A beloved father and soulmate to Tina died 19th November 2017'. The representation of a pint of Guinness is at the foot of this headstone featuring Eddie's signature above the words 'Drank in Belfast'. The base of the headstone states 'Goodnight and joy be with you all', the closing line of 'The Parting Glass', a traditional Scottish song, also long-sung in Ireland, and enjoying considerable popularity to this day, most recently covered by Ed Sheeran.

Michael Grattan - V-2090 - 'in loving memory of Michael (Gerry, Sprungdog, Crazyhorse) March 3 1952 - April 16 2020 Loving Father, Grandfather and Brother. As I walk through the valley of the shadow of death I shall fear no evil'. At the base of the headstone is the representation of a full pint of Harp, with an actual can of the same sitting on the bottom of the headstone. On occasions, the can is also accompanied by a pint glass containing beer, presumably Harp.

Trail 2 – World Tour

This second trail is sponsored by my brother Andrew which is appropriate as he's the family member who has clocked up the most air miles, currently residing in the Grand Duchy of Luxembourg.

This globetrotting trail features folks who lived in, and in some cases are buried in, every corner of the world, and are commemorated on headstones in Roselawn Cemetery.

William James Hutchinson - S-282 - California - '1893 - 1921 interred Live Oak Memorial Park California'. Interred in this grave is William's 'beloved wife' Sarah Rebecca Hutchinson who was living at 3 Sandhurst Gardens, Belfast when she died on 30 August 1979 aged 90, and William Shields Beck who was living at 34 Hillfoot Street, Belfast when he died on 30 November 1978 aged 57, although the latter is not recorded on this headstone.

Alexander Stothard Breeze - D-1754 - India - 'died 3rd August 1955 aged 64. Late Missionary to India'. Breeze was living at 27 Cyprus Gardens, Belfast when he died aged 64, with his wife Catherine Allen Breeze living at 19 Cheswick Road, Acton, London when she died on 3 November 1969 aged 80.

Eric Wilson Anderson - D-749 - Vancouver, Canada - 'dearly loved husband of Moureen died result of an accident Vancouver Canada 4 Oct. 1956 aged 29 years'. Anderson's address at the time of his death was 3227 Renfrew Street, Vancouver, British Columbia and he was buried in Roselawn on 11 October 1956, exactly one week after his death.

Ernest McIntosh - C-723 - Dar es-Salaam - 'Died 16th Oct. 1960 Chief Officer M.N. Interred in Dar es Salaam'. Dar es Salaam, translated as the Place of Peace, is the largest city and former capital of Tanzania. It is the largest city in East Africa and the seventh largest in Africa, with a population of almost seven million people. Located on the

Swahili coast, Dar es Salaam is an important economic centre and one of the fastest growing cities in the world. Buried in this grave is James Easton McIntosh who died on 25 December 1961 aged 39, Ellen McIntosh who died on 26 March 1967 aged 68, and James Easton McIntosh senior who died on 22 May 1967 aged 72, all whilst recorded as living at 12 Sydenham Crescent, Belfast.

Sergeant Laurence Dixon - C-2416 - Singapore - 'R.A.F. Died 2nd July 1965 aged 38 at R.A.F. Changi, Singapore'. Dixon's address was recorded as 3 Sennet Drive, Singapore, and he was interred in Roselawn on 22 July 1965, almost three weeks after his untimely death. Also buried in this grave is 'Phyllis [a] much loved wife, mother and grandmother died 21st July 2017 aged 82'.

Guardsman Allister Cornett - S-219 - Aden - 'died 30th January 1967 Interred in Aden'. Aden is a port city with a population of approximately 800,000 people and, since 2015, the city was the temporary capital of Yemen, located by the eastern approach to the Red Sea (the Gulf of Aden). Interred in this grave is Allister's father Samuel Cornett who died on 22 December 1978 aged 55, and his mother Maisie Cornett who died on 29 January 1989 aged 67, both whilst living at 40 Breda Road, Belfast.

Arthur Howard - F-106 - Rhodesia - this headstone commemorates Arthur Howard 'who died 7th June 1969. Interred in Rhodesia'. Buried in this grave is Arthur's wife Rachel Howard who was living at 48 Stirling Avenue, Castlereagh when she died on 4 April 1969 aged 74, and their son-in-law Alexander Johnston who was living at 45 Ferris Bay Road, Islandmagee when he died on 17 October 1994 aged 66. It strikes me as unusual that the Howards died within a couple of months of each other but are not buried together, so I can only surmise that, after the death of his wife, Arthur moved abroad, possibly to live with one of their children, but died shortly afterwards, and is buried in Rhodesia (now called Zimbabwe).

Ida Wright Kazmayer - T-1354 - United States - 'born 21st May 1920 Died 18th November 1970 Goodnight sweet princess, may the angels sing thee to thy rest'. At the base of this headstone is a symbol for the 'Daughters of the American revolution', a lineage-based membership service organisation for women who are directly descended from a person involved in the United States' efforts towards independence.

Margaret McKelvie - S-3445 - Murchison, South Africa - 'Born 28th January 1910 Born again November 1928 Called home 20th February 1977. Former Matron of Murchison hospital, S.Africa, where she faithfully served the Lord from 1936-1968, and by whom this stone is erected in affectionate and grateful remembrance. Our sister...a servant of the church...A succourer of many. Romans 18 1-2'. Murchison hospital is situated approximately 13 kilometers from Port Shepstone on the deep South Coast of Natal. In the early days of 1928, the Founder of the hospital, Dr Barton, used to ride out on horse-back to attend his patients in their mud huts. However, many came to see him in his own mud hut, and this was the start of what became known as "KwaBathini" - The Place of Barton. The doctor was eventually granted land by the Chief, and in 1928 erected a wood and corrugated iron building, which housed 6 beds on the site of the present hospital. This was the beginning of Murchison Hospital. In 1935 Margaret

arrived at the hospital, later becoming the first matron. Margaret was living at 38 Wanstead Road, Dundonald when she died aged 67.

David Wilkinson - T-563 - Belize - 'Cpl David Cyril Wilkinson R.I.R died 4th March 1978 aged 22 years at Belize'. Belize, formerly known as British Honduras, is a Caribbean country located on the northeastern coast of Central America. Its population of 408,487 in 2019, means that it has the lowest population and population density in Central America, but the country's population growth rate of 1.87% per year is the second highest in the region and one of the highest in the western hemisphere. Wilkinson's home address was recorded as 16 Brenda Street, Belfast, with his cremated remains interred on 15 March 1978. Also buried in this plot is Wilkinson's grandfather Cyril H Armitage who was living at 6 Steens Row, Belfast when he died on 28 October 1971 aged 65, and his grandmother Annie Armitage who was living at 35 Hollycroft Avenue, Belfast when she died on 10 March 1992 aged 82.

Maud Elizabeth Hannah Finch - U-956 - Rangoon - 'Born Rangoon 26th Oct. 1897 Died Glasgow 27th Sept. 1980'. Rangoon, literally translated from Burmese as 'End of Strife', also known as Yangon, is the largest city of Myanmar (also known as Burma). Previously the capital of Myanmar, with over 5 million people, Rangoon is the country's most populous city and its most important commercial centre. Finch was living at 2 Cleveden Crescent, Glasgow at the time of her death aged 82. Also buried in this plot is her husband George William Finch 'Born at Erdington 29th March 1899 Died at Belfast 14th October 1969' aged 70, whilst registered as living at 80 South Parade, Belfast. Erdington is a suburb and ward of Birmingham that is historically part of Warwickshire. The base of this headstone contains the words 'Well done thou good and faithful servant'.

Florence and Brian Cathcart Rankin - V-1704 - Portugal - 'died on holiday [in] Portugal October 1982'. The sole occupant of this grave appears to be Kathleen Margaret Rankin who was living at 508 Upper Newtownards Road, Belfast when she died on 9 February 1984 aged 44.

It looks like Kathleen was the Rankins' daughter, dying less than 18 months after her parents.

Peter McConnell - V-2326 - Hong Kong - 'died 16th Dec. 1983, aged 22, in Hong Kong'. McConnell's address was given as c/o Police Headquarters, Hong Kong at the time of his death, and he was buried in this plot on 31 December 1983. Also buried in this grave is Adeline McConnell who died on 20 January 2002 aged 72, and Vincent James McConnell who died on 5 October 2005 aged 75, both whilst registered as living at 13 Burnside Avenue, Castlereagh.

Dr John Stewart Bell, F.R.S - V-1107 - Geneva - 'died Geneva 1st October 1990 Interred St George's Cemetery Geneva'. Dr Bell is regarded as one of the 20th century's greatest physicists, and was widely believed to have been in line for a Nobel Prize in Physics when he died from a stroke. Bell's Theorem demonstrated that Einstein's views on quantum mechanics were incorrect. First published on 4 November 1964, his theory continues to have a lasting impact on modern physics, and is said to have laid the foundation for quantum information technology. Bell attended Belfast Technical High School, now Belfast Metropolitan College, and then entered Queen's University. The building that once housed the old College, commonly known as the 'Tech', has been renamed John Bell House, whilst the street behind the new Belfast Metropolitan College in Titanic Quarter is called Bell's Theorem Crescent. Bell went on to teach at CERN, Europe's particle physics laboratory near Geneva, Switzerland, with

Professor Mary Daly, President of the Royal Irish Academy, describing Bell as 'one of the most important scientists in the world'. Buried in this plot is John's father, John Bell senior, who died on 2 March 1993 aged 86, and his mother Annie Bell who died on 25 August 2002

aged 96, both whilst living at 240 Tates Avenue, Belfast (the location of a blue plaque in memory of their astounding son).

Jim Moore - R-4049 - Korea - 'Ex. R.U.R. [Royal Ulster Rifles] Korea Died 16th October 1992'. The 1st Battalion, Royal Ulster Rifles disembarked at Pusan in early November 1950 as part of the 29th Independent Infantry Brigade Group for service in the Korean War. They were transported forward to Uijeongbu where, under the direct command of the Eighth United States Army, they were initially directed against North Korean guerrilla forces. Jim was living at Ashleigh House Nursing Home, 12 Linden Road, Bedford when he died aged 63, and was buried on 27 October 1992. Also buried in this plot, but not commemorated on the headstone, is Robert Hamilton who was living at 8 Ardgowan Street, Belfast when he died on 14 January 2010 aged 81. The base of this black, heart-shaped headstone states 'Love is all'.

Raymond Mark Martin - V-538 - Holland - this headstone commemorates a 'beloved grandson Mark Son of Rosemary killed in Holland', whilst living at Lisse, Amsterdam, when he died aged 22 on 14 February 1993, and was buried on 19 February 1993. Also buried in this plot is Samuel Johnston who was living at 21 Wandsworth Road, Belfast when he died on 25 March 1980 aged 59, and Mary Doreen Johnston who was living at 13 Skipperstone Park, Bangor when she died on 20 July 1996 aged 76.

Jim Pollock - S-3781 - New Zealand - Pollock 'died in New Zealand 4th April 1999 - aged 57 years', and it appears that he was buried out there too. Interred in this plot is Margaret Pollock who was living at 60 Templemore Street, Belfast when she died on 9 December 1991 aged 84, and Archibald Pollock who was living at the same address when he died on 4 May 1992 aged 87.

McConnell - Y-2152 - Haiti - this headstone commemorates 'Rev Patrick McConnell 10.6.1935 - 6.11.2005' as well as his 'beloved son Patrick 'Ti Paddy' 10.6.1962 - 5.4.1971 both interred in Haiti'. Buried in this grave is 'Olga McConnell nee Trouillot devoted wife, mother and grandmere 19.5.1931 - 24.2.2017'. Reading between the lines, it seems that Olga was born in Haiti where she married Rev McConnell and gave birth to a son Patrick before moving to Northern Ireland following their respective deaths, and she appears to be the only interment in this grave.

Isabella Milliken - S-975 - Canada - 'passed away in Canada 13th January 2006 aged 101 years'. Milliken's address at the time of her death was Sunnyhill Wellness Centre 217-1402 Eighth Avenue, Northwest Calgary, Alberta, Canada, with her cremated remains interred in this plot on 30 September 2006. Also interred in this grave is Isabella's husband Walter Edmund Milliken who was living at 62 Clonduff Drive, Castlereagh Road, Belfast when he died on 11 March 1976 aged 72. This headstone also contains a strange image, which appears to be a 'rock hand'.

Maurice Wilson McDowell - T-4214 - Pretoria - 'died 23rd May 2008 at his home in Pretoria, South Africa', aged 63 with a home address of 89 Jacobson Drive, Pretoria. Also buried in this grave is Jean McDowell of 104 Larkfield Road, Belfast who died on 8 August 1975 aged 62, and Alexander McDowell who was also living at 104 Larkfield Road when he died on 6 June 1979 aged 77.

Aktar Ali - W-4001 - Bangladesh - 'Precious Memories of our dear son Aktar Ali (Bablu) Born 21st February 1986 Died 24th July 2008' aged 22 whilst living at 16 Priory Park, Newtownards. The base of the headstone reads 'Vill. Chuto Dhirarai, Osmani-Nagar, Sylhet, Bangladesh', presumably his family's home address back in Bangladesh.

Trail 3 – Children

Trail 3 is sponsored by my ever-supportive parents, Glen and Margaret McCabe.

This trail features 21 children, under the age of 18, who tragically died young – not the most uplifting of the chapters in this book.

Noble - D-1730 - Florence (14), Wilhelmina (12), James (8), Isobel (7) and Robert (4) were five children from the same family who died as a result of a gas leak at their home at 50 Thistle Street, Belfast on 7 July 1955. Their impressive double headstone, which would have been amongst the earliest of the headstones erected at Roselawn, states 'our children are gone and we are left, the loss of them to mourn. But we may hope to meet again with Christ before His throne'.

Rhoda McClune - D-547 - 'in precious and everlasting memory of our beloved daughter Roberta (Rhoda), lent to us for 7 years, the sunshine of our home, recalled by the father 30th April 1958'. On top of the headstone is a child angel, above the words 'A little child shall lead them'. Rhoda was living at 54 Hornby Street, Belfast when she died, whilst also buried in this plot is 'her dear father Robert died 17th May 1995. And her loving mother Sarah Margaret (Peggy), died 19th July 2015', with the base of the headstone stating 'Love you forever'.

Nickell - E-471 - 'in loving memory of our darling and only sons Brian [recorded online as Edmund Sheppard Nickell] died 24th March 1961 aged 24 years [and] Alfred died 1935, aged 1 year 7 months'. The boys' parents are also buried in this plot with Mary Jane Nickell dying on 16 January 1962 aged 51, and James Alfred Nicholl dying on 24 April 1971 aged 66, with the three committals (Alfred was buried elsewhere as he died before Roselawn opened) in this grave recorded as living at 44 Parkgate Crescent, Belfast at the time of their deaths.

Allan Moore - U-2443 - below a sister of Allan's, Karen Blaney, recalls her memories of her brother's death: 'Allan was the fifth child of my family. He was born with a hole in his heart in 1963. The famous Dr Pantridge, who invented the defibrillator, devised an operation where he thought he could repair the hole. Allan was the first child to have the operation, but sadly he died during the surgery. The remaining patients, all men, survived going on to live healthy lives. It was heartbreaking. Life for my parents and our family was never the same again. Allan is now dead more than 50 years, but the pain never leaves'. This headstone was erected 'in loving memory of our darling son Allan Lee [Moore]  died 30th May 1969 aged 6 years', whilst living at 40 The Straight, Cregagh. Also commemorated on the headstone is 'his devoted mother Edna Rebecca died 4th October 1991' aged 59 whilst also living at 40 The Straight, 'and dear father, loving husband Cecil Moore died 31st January 2010' aged 82 whilst living at 2d Woodstock House, Belfast, with the base of the headstone stating 'In Heavenly love abiding'.

Joan Scott - T-300 - 'Died 30th May 1972 result of gunshot wounds in her 12th year'. Joan, of 49 Ballymoney Street, Belfast, died three days after being shot by the Irish Republican Army (IRA) during a sniper attack on a Royal Ulster Constabulary (RUC) mobile patrol in the Oldpark Road area of Belfast. The Scott family had emigrated to Liverpool in 1971 but Joan had come back to visit Belfast because she was homesick, and was shot whilst walking with a 13 year old friend who was injured.

Brian McDermott - T-3497 - this headstone commemorates 'Brian Douglas McDermott brutally murdered September 1973 aged 10 years.

Always remembered', with the base of the headstone stating 'Donated by the people of Northern Ireland'. Brian's body was found in the River Lagan one week after he disappeared from Ormeau Park on 2 September. No-one was ever convicted of the murder of Brian, who lived at 40 Well Street, Belfast, with the murder shocking the local community even though it occured in 1973 during the height of 'The Troubles'.

Edward Smith - T-2132 - 'in loving memory of our dear son Edward (Ted) died as result of an accident 29th March 1973 aged 18 years' whilst recorded as living at 5a Ariel Street, Belfast. Tragically much of the text from Ted's grave is replicated in the commemoration of Robert Moreland on the neighbouring headstone - T-2133 - erected 'in loving memory of our dear son Robert (Bobby) died as result of an accident 29th March 1973 aged 18 years' whilst living at 64 Belgrave Street, Belfast, with a flower pot commemorating 'Bobby loving boyfriend of Eileen'. Both 18-year-olds were killed when a car they were travelling in crashed into a lamp-post on the Forth River Road in the Glencairn estate, Belfast. Four girls who were in the car survived the accident.

Hilary Faulkner - T-3084 - 'in loving memory of our darling daughter Hilary Karen died as result of an accident 14th April 1973 aged 13 years', whilst registered as living at 118 Connsbrook Avenue, Belfast. Hilary was participating in a charity walk to raise funds for Strand Presbyterian Church and the Christian Endeavour when she was knocked down and killed on the Ballyregan Road, Dundonald. 23-year-old William Derek Ian Robinson of Torrin Walk, Ballybeen was later convicted of causing Hilary's death as a result of driving with excess alcohol. Also buried in this plot is Hilary's 'Grandmother Martha Ferris died 17th December 1976' aged 53 whilst living at 83 Owenroe Drive, Bangor.

Gibson - S-4134 - 7-year-old Julie Gibson, and her 9-year-old sister Angela, died, along with their mother Lorraine, 29, in the Maysfield Leisure Centre fire on 14 January 1984. Three other people also died in the fire, with the blaze breaking out in a storeroom, and victims overcome by toxic fumes released by smouldering gymnastic mats. The Gibsons, who lived in Holland Drive in east Belfast, are remembered on a simple heart-shaped black headstone as 'At home with the Lord'. Buried close to the Gibsons - S-4164 - is David Bates who 'died in the Maysfield Leisure Centre fire 14th Jan 1984 aged 16 years 3 mths' whilst registered as living at 20 Springvale Park, Belfast. Another victim, Cecil White, 64, lived just a few doors from the Gibsons in Holland Drive, whilst the other victim was James Smyth, 33, of Glenview Park, Belfast.

Natasha Charmaine Kelly Legge - S-1007 - this headstone commemorates 'Natasha C.K. Precious daughter of Marty and Patricia Also brothers and sisters. Can't wait to see your angel face in heaven that will be the place. Good night and God bless our little one 12-9-85 to 17-2-89'. Natasha was aged 3 and was living at 19 Carncaver Road, Belfast at the time of her death. An image of Natasha features on the headstone, with another child - Ross John Pauley - also featuring on the headstone as 'Born 4th April 1979 Died 9th April 1979. Safe in the arms of Jesus', dying, aged 5 days, whilst registered as living at 14 Downshire Park South, Belfast.

Keri Matthews - R-1719 - throughout the cemetery are a number of plaques from a few local hospitals, dedicated to stillborn or young babies. For example, at Plot R-1719, there is a plaque 'In memory of stillborn babies in the Ulster Hospital'. Online records for this plot indicate that the following babies are buried at this plot; Keri Matthews whose address was registered as 4 Orby Mews, Belfast when she was stillborn on 16 March 1989 (and is commemorated on a separate plaque as 'Born asleep 16th March 1989. Sleep little one sleep'); Jan McDowell who was living at 12 Tillysburn Park, Belfast when she died on 26 June 1989 aged 6 days; Lisanne Thackway who was living at 174 Upper Newtownards Road, Belfast when she died on 15 November 1989 aged 3 months; John Gareth Wesley McAvoy of 11 Lothian Avenue, Tullycarnet who died on 30 December 1989 aged 1 day; and a 'Child Of Amanda Prestrew' who was registered as living at

8 Windermere Crescent, Bangor when they died on 4 December 2002 '16 Wks Gest' (16 weeks gestation). Heartbreaking. At the back of the crematorium, beside the Garden of Remembrance, is an area marked by a large stone stating 'Babies Garden of Remembrance. For All Our Babies, Sadly Missed. Loved and Remembered Always'.

Glenn Robinson - R-1139 - Glenn was stillborn on 25 June 1990 when his parents were living at 16 Strathearn Mews, Belfast, with the base of this headstone stating 'A tiny flower just lent not given, to bud on earth and bloom in heaven'. Buried in the neighbouring grave - R-1138 - is Margaret Glenn who was living at 37 Irwin Crescent, Belfast when she died on 7 March 1986 aged 94, and Ellen Glenn who died on 25 August 1989 aged 87 whilst also living at 37 Irwin Crescent.

Stephanie Corrigan - R-3758 - this headstone commemorates 'Precious memories of Stephanie a beloved daughter and sister died 22nd March 1991 aged 22 months' whilst living at 128 Alliance Parade, Belfast. The base of the headstone states 'night night duck a duck', with the representation of a duck at the bottom of the stone.

Darren Newberry - R-3636 - this headstone was erected 'in loving memory of our dear son Darren Died 29th Oct. 1992 aged 6½ years', with the headstone containing the Liverpool Football Club crest and what looks like the Ghostbusters logo. Darren was living at 14 Highpark Drive, Belfast at the time of his death, with a plaque 'from your brothers Kenneth and Jamie' at the foot of the headstone stating 'Two tired eyes are sleeping Two little hands are still The one we lost and loved dear brother is now sleeping in God's will. Our family chain is broken Things will never be the same Until God calls us one by one Till we're a family again'.

Leanne Murray - S-522 - Leanne was aged 13 when she was killed on 23 October 1993 as a result of the Shankill Road bombing, one of the most notorious incidents of the Troubles. Ten people were killed including one of the IRA bombers, a UDA member, Leanne and seven Protestant civilians, with more than fifty people wounded. Leanne lived at 66 Silvio Street, Belfast at the time of her death, and is commemorated on a mural at the junction of the Newtownards Road and Derwent Street, Belfast. Another child who died as a result of the bombing was 7-year-old Michelle Baird who died, along with her parents, and she features in Trail 12.

David William Hunter - P-1113 - David is commemorated on this headstone as '29th Nov. 1978 - 17th Jan. 1995' and was living at 29 Lochinver Drive, Tullycarnet when he died aged 16. David was a son of my long-time partner in crime at the local elections, Billy Hunter, who has been keeping me right for years now. Tragically, also commemorated on this headstone, is David's Mum and Billy's wife 'Margaret Elizabeth (Beth) 29th Oct. 1955 - 4th Jan 2006' who was living at 128 Ardcarn Drive, Belfast when she died aged 50. The base of the headstone features the word 'Endex', military jargon / radio speak for 'End exercise', a display of Billy's sense of humour stating that when you've reached Roselawn, your journey is over.

Richard Hutchinson - P-275 - the roundabout at the main entrance of the cemetery is the Richard Hutchinson Roundabout with a plaque stating 'This Flower Bed is dedicated to the memory of Richard Hutchinson Aged 14 8th May 1981 - 27th July 1995. Someone very

This Flower Bed is dedicated to the memory of
Richard Hutchinson
Aged 14
8th MAY 1981 - 27th JULY 1995
Someone Very Special

special'. Richard was living at 31 Glenholm Park, Four Winds, Belfast at the time of his death, with his headstone commemorating 'A special son, brother and grandson Richard fell asleep 27th July 1995 Aged 14 years', with the base of the headstone stating 'Lean On Me'.

Barkley - P-3194 - 'Precious memories of our beloved sons Robert Paul Born 17th April 1996 Died Tragically 14th April 2001 [and] Gareth William Born 22nd March 1997 Died Tragically 14th April 2001. The angels sang Amazing Grace, the Lord came down and touched their faces, then he whispered sweet and low, come on wee sons it's time to go'. Plaques, with photos of each of the boys, at the base of the headstone state 'Robert God Bless You Son XXX' and 'Gareth God Bless You Son XXX'. Four-year-old brothers Robert and Gareth died in a non-malicious house fire at their home at 4 Sydney Street West, Belfast. The boys were trapped in the house when the blaze broke out just after 7am in an upstairs front bedroom where the two little boys were found. The boys' parents and two siblings survived the tragedy.

David Ellson - P-4107 - born on 28 August 1999, David was aged two when he died of meningitis on 16 February 2002 whilst living in Dundonald, and was laid to rest on 1 March 2002. This headstone contains a lovely photo of a smiling David, accompanied by the words 'A very special son and brother. All he ever knew was love', with the base of the headstone commemorating "Our Wee Man". David was the youngest son of Maureen and James, and brother of Conor. My friend James is a tour Guide with the award-winning DC Tours, sponsors of Chapter 11.

Baby Ellie McKee - W-378 - this small headstone at a well-tended grave incorporates the image of a teddy bear, and reads '13th October 2006. Sweet dreams our little angel Love always Mummy & Daddy XOXO', with a plaque at the base remembering a 'Grand-daughter. God's garden needed a little flower'. Ellie was a child of a niece of my family friend Nan Woodburn and was tragically stillborn on 13 October 2006, whilst her parents were registered as living at 8a Grahamsbridge Road, Dundonald.

Hauley Elizabeth Fullerton - R-1059 - a heart-shaped plaque at the foot of this headstone commemorates Hauley, with a photo of the infant, along with the following verse: 'One year one month and five days is a little life cut short. One year, one month and five days love for a lifetime. Love always Mummy & Daddy'. Hauley died on 11 November 2009 aged 13 months, whilst registered as living at 115 Newcastle Road, Kilkeel. Commemorated on the family headstone is William Beck who was living at 72 Benburb Street, Belfast when he died on 4 September 1985 aged 65, Marjorie Beck who was living at the same address when she died on 21 June 2005 aged 79, and Sylvia Stevenson who was also living at 115 Newcastle Road, Kilkeel when she died on 29 November 2011 aged 51.

Trail 4 – Fabulous Females

This trail is sponsored by Dr Jacqueline Granlees who initially suggested a 'women only' tour of Dundonald Cemetery to me, and has also supported the relevant trail in my previous books.

This trail tells 'herstory' rather than 'history', and includes one of the most fantastic woman ever, my Granny Craig.

Christina Wilson - D-548 - 'In loving memory of my dear wife and our devoted mother Christina who was killed on the 22nd March 1958', with the base of the headstone reading 'In our hearts she will live forever'. Wilson was fatally injured when knocked down by a car on the Holywood Road, Belfast whilst crossing the road with her husband on the morning of 22 March. Christina was living nearby at 54 Connsbrook Avenue, Belfast when she died, and appears to be the only interment in this plot.

Susan Chisholm - E-158 - in 1897 Susan married Roderick Chisholm in Lisburn. Roderick was born in Dumbarton on 20 December 1868 and was at the forefront in the design of *Olympic* and *Titanic*. One of Titanic's nine-strong Guarantee Group, like the rest of his counterparts, 43-year-old Roderick died in the sinking. Susan was living at 6 Sandford Avenue, Belfast at the time of her husband's death, and was still living there when she died on 22 February 1961 aged 87. A plaque at the bottom of the avenue commemorates Roderick, who is remembered on the book-shaped headstone as dying during the 'Titanic disaster 15th April 1912', with the second 'page' of the headstone stating 'Peace perfect peace'. Also commemorated on this headstone is a son, James Chisholm, who died on 18 September 1960 aged 61 whilst also living at 6 Sandford Avenue. Belfast Titanic Society President Susie Millar recently moved into this property. Susie's great-grandfather died in the sinking of the Titanic, so it is fitting that the Titanic link to 6 Sandford Avenue continues to this day.

Elizabeth Frost - E-555 - this headstone commemorates Elizabeth who 'died on 23 February 1961' aged 72, whilst living at 2 Hillcrest Gardens, Belfast. Elizabeth was the wife of Anthony (Artie) Frost who, like Roderick Chisholm mentioned previously, worked on both *Olympic* and *Titanic*, supervising the fitting of machinery. Frost was another member of the Titanic Guarantee Group, with a plaque to commemorate him at the end of Sunbury Avenue, close to Sandford Avenue as mentioned previously. Interestingly, Elizabeth died one day after Susan Chisholm, with the final resting places of the two Titanic widows within a few yards of each other. Artie is commemorated on the base of the family headstone as 'lost on Titanic 1912'. Artie and Elizabeth's daughter Marjorie was President of the Ulster Titanic Society until her death in 1995. Artie's father, George William Frost, is buried in an unmarked grave - E4-580 - in Dundonald, and features in Trail 3: Harland & Wolff of my book about the cemetery.

Celena Blanchflower - E-418 - Celena (known as *Cis*) was the mother of footballing brothers Jackie and Danny Blanchflower, and was living at 1 Kings Brae, Knock when she died on 9 September 1974 aged 72. Predeceased by her husband John - 'a devoted husband and father' - who died at 7 Ballycraigy Ring, Larne on 5 June 1961 aged 63, Cis was apparently a useful footballer in her time, captaining Bloomfield Ladies team. Cis's eldest son Jackie played for Manchester United on 117 occasions winning two league titles, and 12 Northern Ireland caps, before his career was cut short due to injuries sustained in the Munich air disaster. Danny captained Tottenham Hotspur in the 1960s when they won the League, the FA Cup and European Cup Winners' Cup, and also made 56 appearances as a Northern Ireland international, later managing the team. According to another son William, who I had the pleasure of speaking to on the phone in 2020, the Blanchflower brothers gained their sporting prowess from their mother, a fact confirmed by Danny himself in an article entitled 'My Mother Was An Inside Right'. Again, according to William, a sister of his father played football along with his mother, and that is apparently how the two first met.

Ruby Esme Mitchell - S-1035 - 'daughter of the late Mr and Mrs R.A. Mitchell of Marmont, Strandtown died 30th September 1976' aged 73 whilst living at 49 Malone Park, Belfast. In 1886 Robert Armstrong Mitchell acquired 'Marmont' for £4,000, the house containing four reception rooms, a billiard room, seven bedrooms and three servants bedrooms. In 1955 'Marmont' was offered to the Northern Ireland Council for Orthopaedic Development for potential use as a school for disabled young people, with the school opening on 20 November 1961 as Mitchell House School, now a co-educational special school for children with physical disabilities. The Esme Mitchell Trust, administered by Cleaver Fulton Rankin, supports charitable projects of a cultural or artistic nature, which includes grants to museums, churches and preservation trusts.

Norma Spence - S-508 - 'Woman Search Officer Norma Spence Served Belfast & Londonderry Murdered Whilst On Duty By The Provisional I.R.A. 3 March 1978' aged 25 whilst registered as living at 3 Arran Park, Ballybeen, Dundonald. Spence was shot dead while at an Army pedestrian checkpoint at Donegall Street, Belfast. The Civilian Search

Unit (C.S.U) Northern Ireland logo is at the top of this headstone, with a plant pot at the base of the headstone 'from her friends in the C.S.U'. Also interred in this plot is 'a dear Mum and Granny Letty Spence 14.6.1930 - 6.11.2014'.

Alice Morrow - V-1431 - the grandmother of Stewart McCracken (sponsor of two chapters in this book), Alice was living at 62 Rathmore Street, Belfast when she died on 29 August 1982 aged 77, with her husband, Stewart's grandfather, Stewart Morrow living at 14 Mount Street South, Belfast when he died on 25 November 1988 aged 85. Also interred in this plot is a son, William John Morrow, who was living at 10 Clara Avenue, Belfast when he died on 2 May 1993 aged 66.

Grace Bannister O.B.E. - R-1358 - 'a loving wife, mother and grandmother died 5th December 1986 Lord Mayor of Belfast 1981 - 1982'. Educated at Roslyn Street Primary School and Park Parade, leaving school at 14 to work in the family bakery, during the Second World War Grace went to work at Mackie's making parts for Stirling bombers. Bannister was elected to Belfast Corporation in 1965, representing the Ulster Unionist Party, and served as Deputy Lord Mayor of Belfast in 1975-1976, and in 1979 was appointed High Sheriff of Belfast. In 1981 she was elected as the first female Lord Mayor of Belfast, beating Paddy Devlin, as featured in the next trail. Awarded an OBE in the 1984 New Year Honours for services to local government, Grace was living at 34 Grand Parade, Belfast when she died on 5 December 1986 aged 62. Grace's husband John was also living at 34 Grand Parade when he died on 30 March 1993 aged 73.

Lorraine McCausland - 'beloved mother of Stuart and Craig murdered 8th March 1987 aged 23 years'. Police believe Ms McCausland, who had been on a night out, was raped in a Loyalist club at Tyndale, Belfast before she was savagely beaten and her body dumped beside a stream in Forthriver, Belfast. 18 years later Lorraine's son Craig Charles (CC), who was aged just two when she was killed, 'a devoted daddy [was himself] murdered 11th July 2005 aged

20 years', after being shot in Dhu Varren Park in North Belfast with the killing blamed on tensions within loyalism.

Alice May Wilkinson - V-1082 - 'died 15th May 1987. For 50 years a dedicated Sunday School teacher also friend and helper of Presbyterian Orphan Society'. Wilkinson was living at Flat 15, Fitzroy Court, Belfast at the time of her death, aged 89.

Lily (Elizabeth) Boal - V-1473 - 'Died 10th August 1987. Ex Missionary WEC'. WEC International is an interdenominational mission agency of evangelical tradition which focuses on evangelism, discipleship and church planting through music and the arts, serving addicts and vulnerable individuals throughout the world. Elizabeth was living at 56 Mountcollyer Avenue, Belfast when she died aged 77.

Edith Gough - R-273 - my Aunt Edith was my Granda's McCabe's sister and, bizarrely, also my Granny Craig's best friend. It was Edith who organised my Mum and Dad's first meeting when they were both babies! Sadly Edith, a 'devoted wife and mother' died on 14 September 1987 aged 66 whilst living at 32 Creevy Avenue, Braniel, Belfast. Her husband Harry (Henry Thomas Gough, as my Granda always used to call him), 'a much loved father', was living at Stormont Care Home, 8 Summerhill Avenue, Belfast when he died on 3 February 2008 aged 88. In my forthcoming *Hundred Houses of East Belfast* book, Edith and Harry's youngest son Stephen recalls his happy upbringing at 32 Creevy Avenue.

Jane (Jean) Craig - R-3295 - my wonderful Granny Craig died after a stoical fight against a rare form of cancer on 9 October 2001 aged 81, with my old chum and Granda James Vincent (Vinty) Craig dying on 21 December 2003 aged 88, both registered as living at 5 Kensington Avenue, the same house where they lived for 57 years. There's hardly a day goes by when I don't think fondly of my Granny, and it saddens me slightly that I've only got interested in her life 'pre-Granny' since she died. So, for example, I have now tracked down the grave in Dundonald Cemetery where a family killed at 1 Hatton Drive during the Belfast blitz are buried, whilst my Granny sheltered under the stairs nearby at number 30. On a number of occasions, I've also visited the Mayes grave at Knocknamuckley, county Armagh where my Granny's grandparents are buried. A favourite of many happy memories I have of my Granny Craig was when I was eating my tea at her house one evening (almost certainly a Thursday) and, as we were chatting, and not realising that the lid wasn't properly secured, I shook the tomato sauce covering my Granny, who was standing nearby, with the stuff!

Mary Bridget Allison, BEM - V-1609 - a caretaker at Annadale School, Belfast, Allison was awarded the BEM in the Queens Birthday Honours in 1983. Allison was living at 24 Annadale Terrace, Belfast when she died on 19 May 2007 aged 83, having been predeceased by her husband Samuel Allison who died on 21 July 1981 aged 70 whilst also living at 24 Annadale Terrace. Allison is well remembered by Mark Wylie and Paul Donnelly from DC Tours (sponsors of Trail 11), with Paul reminiscing that a teacher once informed students that there were two people who ran the school - Mrs Allison and the Principal, probably in that order.

Helen Lewis, MBE - W-1301 - 'Helen Lewis (née Katz) '22.06.1916 - 31.12.2009'. Born on 22 June 1916 into a German-speaking Jewish family in Trutnov in the Kingdom of Bohemia, Lewis studied dance and philosophy at the German University of Prague and, in 1938, married Paul Hermann, a Czech from a Jewish family. Following the invasion of Czechoslovakia in 1939, the Hermanns were sent to Terezín in 1942 and, in 1944, were transferred to Auschwitz and separated. Paul Hermann died in 1945 on a forced march, not long before the end of the Second World War. Helen, who survived two 'selections' by

Dr Josef Mengele, was later sent to Stutthof concentration camp in northern Poland. Helen's mother, Elsa Katz, who had been deported in 1942, had died at Sobibór extermination camp and is commemorated on this headstone as '10.08.1893 - 1942 (?) A victim of the Holocaust with no known resting place'. After the end of the war Helen began to correspond with Harry Lewis, a Czech with British nationality whom she had known at school, and they married in Prague in the summer of 1947 and in October moved to Belfast. After the birth of her two sons, Michael and Robin, in 1949 and 1954, Lewis began to work as a choreographer, also teaching modern dance, and in 1962 started the Belfast Modern Dance Group. Her book *A Time to Speak* was published in 1992 and was translated into several languages, and then adapted for the theatre by the late, great Sam McCready. In the 2001 Birthday Honours, Helen Lewis was awarded an MBE for her services to contemporary dance. She died at her home, 46 Osborne Drive, Belfast aged 93. Harry Lewis is commemorated on this headstone as '18.02.1909 - 31.12.1991'.

Johanna Maria Murphy - S-759 - '(nee Wilhelmsen) *17.4.94 +11.9.2015 devoted wife, mother and grandmother Goda mamma takk fyri alt' which translates from Norwegian as 'Good mum thanks for everything'. This grave also contains the remains of Stewart Murphy who was living at 2 Islandmore Avenue, Newtownards when he died on 2 March 1981 aged 62, with the base of the headstone stating 'in the garden of happy memories we meet each day'.

Georgina (Ena) McKeown - R-2831 - born on 10 August 1917, a competitive cyclist from a young age, Ena travelled all over the world with her husband on her beloved bicycle. In 1953 she became the first woman to win the Best All Rounder (BAR) cup, also breaking the record for the time it took to cycle from Derry Post Office to Belfast Post Office the same year, completing the

journey in three hours and 46 minutes. The bicycle used to accomplish these feats is now in the Ulster Transport Museum. Ena's husband Billy, a joiner, died on 2 October 1989 aged 66 whilst living at 22c Cloghan Park, Belfast. Speaking on her 100th birthday, Ena said 'It is a long time to be alone' but was grateful for the 'happy memories. We loved children and family but we put cycling in front of that so we never had any'. As well as the many sporting triumphs in her life, Ena survived the Ballymacarrett railway disaster on 10 January 1945 which claimed 19 lives. 'We got on the train, and at Sydenham the train crashed. Everybody on the train was lying about everywhere. They were all shouting 'Watch my legs, my legs, don't walk over me, I can't see you'. I had to go to the Royal Victoria Hospital to be examined but I was so fortunate to survive'. After the incident Ena said that she appreciated her life even more, and credited cycling as the secret to a long life. Ena died on 28 March 2019, aged 101 and 7 months whilst resident in a nursing home in Holywood.

Mollie Cornforth - C-1291 - born in January 1906, Mollie's father Samuel A. Armstrong was a charge hand engineer at Harland & Wolff, taking his 4-year-old daughter Mollie to witness *Titanic's* launch on 30 April 1910. Recalling the launch Mollie stated 'I remember standing on the cobblestones, looking up at the side of this big ship. I could see a lot of people on the deck, and there was so much noise from the crowds'. Mollie died on 12 August 2003 aged 97 whilst living at Breffni Lodge, Wandsworth Road, Belfast, having been predeceased by her first husband Cyril William Menzies Drysdale - who worked in the drawing office at the shipyard - who died at 42 Mount Charles, Belfast on 2 October 1963 aged 60.

Lillian Spence - V 235 - born on New Year's Eve 1898, Lily was living at 64 Beersbridge Road, Belfast when she died on 28 January 2008 aged 109. Predeceased by her husband Edward (Eddie) who was living at 52 Calvin Street, Belfast when he died on 10 July 1979 aged 90, Lily had eight children and, until her death, she lived with one of her daughters next door to Spence's fish and chip shop, which was a family business started by Eddie in 1921. When asked what was her secret of long life, she replied: 'hard work and clean living'. Lily was a member of Willowfield Parish Church and was visited regularly by the Rector at the time, the Rev David McClay, as well as my Mum, when she worked for the Church.

Julie Maxwell-Lewis - Y-2061 - Julie studied for a Degree in Theatre Studies at Ulster University in Coleraine before attending the Royal Welsh College of Music and Drama in Cardiff, where she met her husband to be Rhodri, and they were married on 24 September 2017. Under her professional name Julie Maxwell, she worked with a range of theatre companies; Tinderbox, Bruiser, Replay, Prime Cut, The Lyric, Red Lemon amongst others. She also formed a hugely successful partnership with her friend and fellow  actor Caroline Curran creating Christmas shows for the Theatre at the Mill, Newtownabbey. The two also appeared alongside each other in the BBC comedy show Soft Border Patrol. Julie was in the process of refocusing her career as a Director when she died at the tragically young age of 36 on a night out with her husband. Her death led to the McCann family raising money to have defibrillators installed in a wide range of venues in Belfast.

Trail 5 – Marvellous Men

This trail is sponsored by Julie Roulston and Gail McMullan in memory of their Daddy Alex McMullan, and Mummy Kathleen, as featured later in this section.

In the interests of equality, I am also including a trail featuring only men, including one man I didn't expect to find in Roselawn - Paddy Devlin.

Alfred William Greeves - D-1339 - 'died 14th September 1956 aged 57 years'. Greeves was predeceased by his son, Alfred Henry Malcomson Greeves, who died on 13 October 1954 aged 20, both whilst registered as living at 58 Knocklofty Park, Belfast. Also buried in this plot is 'his wife Sara Rawlinson Greeves died 20th December 1992 aged 88 years' and 'Rose Margretta [Greeves] his daughter died 24th June 1993 aged 60 years', both whilst registered as living at 41 Thornhill Park, Belfast. In my forthcoming *Hundred Houses of East Belfast* book, Dave Stanley recalls his memories of his grandparents' house at 58 Knocklofty Park: 'My grandfather, Alfred Greeves, was at Campbell College with C.S Lewis and his father, also Alfred, built his house on land adjacent to Little Lea after the Lewis brothers moved to England. I loved that house. It was also my introduction to CS Lewis as my grandmother used to read from copies Lewis had given to her, but it always puzzled me why they were signed 'from Jack" (Jack was the name Lewis preferred to be referred to by family and friends).

Alderman Thomas Loftus Cole, CBE JP - D-2095 - 'of Elmfield House Whitewell, Newtownabbey Sometime Member of the Imperial and Northern Ireland Parliaments and High Sheriff and Deputy Lord Mayor of Belfast died 7th March 1961' aged 84. Born in 1877, Cole studied at Sullivan Upper School in Holywood before qualifying as a pharmacist. Despite this, he worked as a property developer, and was elected to Lurgan Urban District Council in 1911, serving until 1917. He returned to politics in 1931, winning a seat on the Belfast Corporation for the Ulster Unionist Party which he held until 1958. He was High Sheriff of Belfast in 1937 and Deputy Lord Mayor of Belfast in 1938-1939. At the 1945 general election, Cole was elected as Member of Parliament for Belfast East until the 1950 election. He also held the seat of Belfast Dock in the Northern Ireland House of Commons from 1949 until he lost the seat in 1953.

Alderman Albert H Duff - E-628 - 'Missionary Sandy Row Belfast for 47 years'. The Belfast City Mission commenced work in the Sandy Row area in 1829. In 1923 the Mission purchased a large hall in Clementine Street with Duff as missionary. Duff was also a Belfast City councillor running as a candidate for the UPA (Ulster Peoples Action) against Brian Maginess in Iveagh at the 1958 Northern Ireland general election, with Duff taking 41.5% of the vote, although he failed to win the seat. Duff was more successful later in 1958 when he regained a seat on Belfast City Council. Duff was next in the headlines in 1967 when, along with Rev. Ian and Eileen Paisley, he left Belfast City Hall in protest at the seats allocated to them at a civic lunch to mark a visit by Princess Margaret. At the time Councillor Duff represented St George's Ward, and was recorded as a City Missionary / Pastor at Aughrim Street Mission Hall in Sandy Row (now affiliated to the Free Presbyterian Church). Known affectionately as 'Daddy Duff', Alderman Duff ran a soup kitchen and carried out other social work during the Depression. Alderman Duff lived at 38 Fitzroy Avenue, Belfast when he died on 15 January 1971 aged 80.

Dr Compton Theodore Denny - T-1626 - Doctor Denny 'died 17th January 1972' aged 68, whilst 'his beloved wife Dorothy May died 22nd July 1982' aged 70, both registered as living at 7 Ardenlee Avenue, Belfast at the time of their deaths. The base of this headstone states 'In heavenly love abiding', with a flower holder remembering 'C.T. Denny, M.D.'. Dr Deeny was a black doctor who practiced in East Belfast for many years, with a surgery at 1 Ballarat Street and then 134 Ravenhill Road. Dr Deeny's son Garnett was born on 19 July 1931, and became a professional heavyweight boxer, fighting from 1946 until 1960, winning 63 bouts (33 by knockout), drawing 18 and losing 5. In later life Garnett owned a newsagency at the junction of Gilnahirk and the Lower Braniel Roads.

Isaac Agnew - V-190 - Agnew was living at Rockfield House, Dundonald when he died on 12 August 1979 aged 80. In the late 1960s Agnew acquired Rockfield, with the building subsequently becoming Rockfield nursing home which closed down around 2010. Rockfield was for sale during 2020, along with grounds of 46 acres, with offers invited in the region of £3 million. Of course, the name Isaac Agnew is still extremely well-known in Belfast in 2021, with the Isaac Agnew motor dealership established in 1931. Also buried in this plot is Isaac's wife, Kathleen Agnew, who was living at 20 Craigarusky Road, Newtownards when she died on 13 May 2006 aged 85.

John Keenan - S-4205 - John was living at 37 Mayflower Street, Belfast when he died on 23 March 1984 aged 63, with Minnie Elizabeth Keenan dying at Orchard House, 2 Cherryvalley Park, Belfast on 28 September 2004 aged 80. John and Minnie's children include Brian who was kidnapped by Shia militiamen in April 1986. Held in increasingly brutal conditions in the suburbs of Beirut and in the Beka'a valley for the next four and a half years, Keenan's story of his abduction and imprisonment is told in his best-selling, award-winning memoir An *Evil Cradling*. Keenan now lives in Dublin with his wife and children. It was a pleasure to meet another of John and Minnie's children, Elayne, on a number of my tours.

Robert 'Bob' Bishop - R-1090 - the man credited with discovering George Best, Bishop was a bachelor living with his sister at 9 Bloomdale Street, Belfast. According to George Best's approved biography *Immortal*, the scout had three hobbies: budgies, Border Collie dogs and, above all, football. A riveter in Harland & Wolff, in his

free time Bishop ran Boyland Youth Club at 46 Lomond Avenue. In 1950 Manchester United appointed him as scout paying him £2 a week plus expenses, also installing a telephone in Bishop's house to communicate with England. In 35 years, Bishop brought more than 100 players to Old Trafford including Best, Jimmy Nicholl, David McCreery, Sammy McIllroy and Norman Whiteside. A distinctive figure, with a cigarette hanging from his lips, and wearing a V-neck sweater in winter and a white shirt in summer, 'The Bishop' also brought young players to Helen's Bay where he rented an austere cottage called 'The Manse' as a base for football camps. Bishop was aged 90 when he died on 13 June 1990, having been predeceased by his sister Kathleen who died on 27 November 1987.

John Torrans - R-2672 - commemorated on the headstone as 'Ex-RAF', John Torrans served with distinction in the RAF during the Second World War. Shot down over France in 1943, he was rescued by the French resistance and hidden for some six months, before finally ending up as a prisoner of war. John, a grandson of one of the founder members of the club in 1886, funded the Torrans Trophy, an award presented annually to a Linfield player deemed by the club's directors to have achieved legendary status. Noel Bailie became the first holder of the Torrans Trophy, with other recipients of the Torrans Award including living Linfield legends Martin McGaughey, Glenn Ferguson, George Dunlop and Peter Rafferty. Tommy Dickson, Sammy Pavis and Joe Bambrick - the remains of all of whom are interred in Roselawn - also previously won the trophy. John was living at 14 Deanby Gardens, Belfast when he died on 5 February 2007 aged 84.

Patrick (Paddy) Joseph Devlin - P-4014 - 'beloved husband and father died 15th August 1999 aged 74 years' whilst registered as living at 457 Oldpark Road, Belfast. Devlin was a founding member of the Social Democratic and Labour Party (SDLP), a former Stormont MP, and a member of the 1974 Power Sharing Executive. Described as a 'relentless campaigner against sectarianism', Devlin had once been a member of the IRA but later renounced physical force republicanism to work at transcending sectarian differences.

Robert Conway - S-1760 - this grave contains the remains of the parents of my long-standing and upstanding friend, Lindsay Conway. Lindsay's mother, Elizabeth Jane (Elsie) Conway, died on 3 April 1977 aged 59 whilst living at 42 Sydenham Gardens, Belfast when Lindsay was aged 24. Lindsay's father Robert worked for 42 years for Stewarts Cash Stores, and Lindsay recalls fondly his father's time working there in the company started by Joseph L Stewart (as featured in my Dundonald Cemetery book). Robert retired from the position of Internal Auditor with Stewarts in 1980. Robert was prominent in the life and witness of Megain Memorial Presbyterian Church, just across the road from Stewart Cash Stores on the Newtownards Road - being elected to the Kirk Session in his late twenties, Sunday School Superintendent and Boy's Brigade Captain. Robert died on 4 December 2000 aged 85, whilst also living at 42 Sydenham Gardens. Robert and Elsie had four children Georgie, Kay, Tom and Lindsay.

Frederick Costley - P-3235 - this headstone was erected 'in loving memory of Frederick a much loved husband devoted father and grandfather Died 28th June 2004' aged 81 whilst living at 4 Cabinhill Gardens, Belfast. Frederick, who worked at Harland & Wolff for many years including during the Belfast blitz of 1941 when he also worked as  an ARP (Air Raid Precautions) Warden in Moira in between shifts in the Yard, was the father of my good friend John Costley. John has been kind enough to sponsor a couple of trails in this publication, and also contributed towards my *Hundred Houses of East Belfast* book, recalling his happy childhood living in Cabinhill Gardens with his father, mother Tillie – who is currently 96 years young, and his brother Charles.

David Robinson, M.B.E. - W-2790 - '18 August 1933 - 26 June 2013 Founder and President of the N.I Transplant Association'. Robinson suffered the first of nine heart attacks in 1971 aged 38, also experiencing a stroke and losing his speech, before a heart transplant in January 1991 at the Freeman Hospital, Newcastle upon Tyne. In an interview on www.nitransplant.org in 2009, Robinson said 'I'm now 75 and it has made such a difference to my life. I continue to walk and cycle and get as much exercise as possible to keep my heart healthy - it came from a 17-year-old donor who died and carried the card. Now, I have two wonderful grandchildren I would never have seen'. A nearby bench also commemorates Robinson as 'always helping others'.

Fergal 'Fergs' O'Mahony - W-2714 - '18th February 1983 - 9th September 2014. Pianist, Composer, Magic Man, "Musical Genius"' with the image of a grand piano at the top of the headstone and the base stating 'Happy music making, happy playing and happy lives' followed by 'Fergal x' as a signature. O'Mahony began studying at the piano from an early age. After studying with the Royal Northern College of Music (RNCM), he went on to study piano on a full scholarship at the Cologne Hochschule für Musik and then the Guildhall School of Music and Drama where he gained his MMus and MMP, both with distinction. As a pianist Fergal performed throughout the UK and Europe, as concerto soloist appearing with the Royal Liverpool Philharmonic Orchestra, Manchester Camerata, Lakewood Symphony Orchestra and several others. He also toured with the European Union Youth Orchestra under Vladimir Ashkenazy. A great lover of the theatre, his first large-scale piece was the musical *Gutter Press* which was completed in early 2012, receiving several 4-star reviews. Fergal then completed the composition of a second musical written with Aoife Nally entitled *Hallowed Ground* before his death aged 31.

Hugh Smyth - W-2880 - 'Alderman Hugh Smyth (OBE) died 12th May 2014'. Born off the Woodvale Road, Belfast in 1941 as one of nine siblings, Smyth worked for Shorts before starting his long political career as an independent unionist in Belfast City Council in 1972. Smyth served in the Assembly of 1973, and was also a key figure in the

Good Friday Agreement negotiations, an experience he described as 'extraordinary'. The Progressive Unionist Party man who served as Lord Mayor of Belfast in 1994 - was the longest serving member of Belfast City Council, and was awarded an OBE in 1996. Party colleague Dr John Kyle described Smyth as a 'pioneer of loyalist politics who worked tirelessly for the welfare of working class communities'. A plaque at the base of the headstone states 'A golden heart stopped beating. Two willing hands are still The one who did so much for me Is resting at God's will XX'.

Colin 'Riot' McQuillan - P-290 - 'beloved partner of Nikki fell asleep 18th Aug. 2014. Loved by all. "We're here for a good time, not a long time"'. Colin formed the punk band Runnin' Riot in the 1990s, and was the singer in the band, dying in his sleep aged 45 in the middle of a UK tour, where the band was supporting Lars Frederksen's Old Firm Casuals. The band's songs included *Lost Generation, Divide & Conquer* and *Drunk & Disorderly*, with fellow band members posting on Facebook, 'Sleep well tonight mate, Marty, Ralph and Eden'. A photo of Colin singing features on the headstone, whilst a bottle of Buckfast rests on the base of the headstone. This headstone also commemorates 'a devoted husband and father' Francis Carson McQuillan who died on 25 January 1995 aged 70, and 'a loving wife and mother' Georgina McQuillan who died on 3 August 2003 aged 85, both whilst registered as living at 145b Belvoir Drive, Belfast.

William 'Plum' Smith - Y-2248 - born in January 1954 in Belfast's Shankill Road area, the first son and one of six children to Charles William Smith, a shipyard worker, and his wife Isobel, Smith spent five years in Long Kesh prison camp, convicted of shooting a Catholic man 18 times, who survived. In prison he learned about Irish history, and was the first loyalist to learn Irish, sitting at a fence and being taught by a Provisional IRA member on the other side. His Irish teacher did not just teach him Irish, but how to make poteen. Smith was in the first group to study for the Open University in Long Kesh. On his release, he worked at Harland and Wolff where he became active in the Amalgamated Transport and General Workers Union (now part of Unite), first as a shop steward, then as convenor, but was dismissed after leading a campaign against privatisation of the shipyard. Chair of the Progressive Unionist Party, Smith is best known as the Chair of the press conference that announced the Combined Loyalist Military Command's ceasefire, and was one of those central to bringing about that ceasefire. Smith died on 8 June 2016 aged 62.

Ivan Foster, MBE - T-198 - 'died 1st March 2017'. Born on 18 November 1927, Foster became a member of Linfield F.C in December 1966, before becoming a life member in 1978. Foster served the club in numerous capacities and was elected to the club's management committee in 1991, serving in the post with distinction until stepping down as a director in May 2015. He was secretary of the ground committee in 1996, and for many years he was the Linfield representative to the County Antrim FA, and served for a period as chairman of the senior clubs committee of the same body. A former secretary of the 1982 True Blues Linfield Supporters' Club, and vice president of 1st Newtownabbey LSC, he was appointed MBE for his services to football. In a tribute, Linfield FC said: 'Ivan Foster was the elder statesman of the club, and a gentleman of great dignity and wisdom. With his trademark bow tie, Ivan added a touch of colour and class to the Windsor Park landscape'. Foster was predeceased by his wife Elizabeth Hilary Foster who was living at 16 Wynchurch Road, Belfast when she died on 13 August 1972 aged 39, with the base of this headstone reading 'our beloved parents together again. Forever in our thoughts'.

Alexander (Alex) McMullan - V-1516 - commemorated on this headstone as a 'dear husband to Kathleen [and] a loving Daddy and Nanda', Alex was the father of regular graveyard tour attendees Julie Roulston and Gail McMullan. Alex first worked with his father in his grocery business, 'Alexs' in Imperial Street, Belfast, working alongside his sister Isabel, making butter from the slab which was then wrapped in greaseproof paper. Alex junior inherited his parents' eye for a business opportunity using his Morris Oxford car to deliver and collect washing machines daily to housewives. Daily rental was half a crown (12.5 pence). By the mid-1960s, Alex junior had sold his parents' business but it remained in the common memory as 'Alex's Grocers Shop'. Alex (junior) died on 30 April 2017 aged 92, with the story of his father and him - fondly known as 'the smart Alexs' - featuring in the  EastSide Partnership's Heritage Lives trail. Also commemorated on this headstone is Kathleen McMullan 'a loving mum and nanny' who died on 13 September 1996 aged 62, like her husband registered as living at 2 Orby Drive, Belfast at the time of her death, and 'her sister Grace (Dixie) Keenan [who] died 29th March 2011' aged 79 whilst living at 6d Ardcarn Park, Belfast.

David Greer - S-3921 - this headstone was erected 'in loving memory of a beloved son and brother David called home 19 February 1999' aged 29, with the base of the headstone stating 'Till We Meet Again'. Davey was a friend of my friends Des Husin and David Hoey, and I remember meeting Davey on a number of occasions. Davey, who was living at 51 Soudan Street, Belfast, when he died, worked for a local stained glass window manufacturer, and a window dedicated to his memory was subsequently installed in St Simons Church of Ireland on the Donegall Road where Davey had previously been a member of the Church Lads Brigade.

Dr Michael Leckenby Allen - W-1607 - born in England and growing up in Wales, Allen joined the English department at Queen's University Belfast in 1965, where he worked as a senior lecturer in American and Irish literature until his retirement in 2001. He was an original member of the 'Belfast Group', the writers' forum that fostered the work, from the mid-1960s onwards, of some of Ireland's leading poets, novelists and playwrights, among them Seamus Heaney, Bernard MacLaverty and Stewart Parker. He also taught the poets Paul Muldoon, Ciaran Carson and Medbh McGuckian when they were undergraduates at Queen's. In *Preoccupations*, Heaney acknowledges Michael Allen as 'the reader over my shoulder'. Muldoon has also paid tribute to Allen as the greatest poetry critic he knew. Michael Allen was, for Longley, and for other poets too, the first and most trusted reader, the man whose subtle and astute judgments on literature were often inspirational. Allen, who was living at 96 Marlborough Park Central, Belfast at the time of his death aged 75, is remembered on his headstone as 'Teacher and Literary Critic 15.XII.1935 - 31.VII.2011 beloved husband of Maureen Allen .... Love is not love Which alters when it alteration finds, Or bends with the remover to remove: O, no! it is an ever fixed mark, That looks on tempests and is never shaken'.

Colm Davis OBE - Y-2460 - the former head teacher at Tor Bank School in Dundonald, Davis died on 27 January 2021 aged 62. The North Belfast man, who was awarded an OBE in June 2017 for services to special education, was diagnosed with Motor Neurone Disease in May 2016. He then used his experience for tireless fundraising and to help raise awareness for the condition through his work with Motor Neurone Disease Association NI. The dad-of-three was a lifelong  Leeds United fan with his son Colm Jnr telling the Yorkshire Evening Post 'My dad was a gold membership holder at Leeds United and we got to as many games as we could. There was nothing that made my Dad happier than watching Leeds United. He was an amazing man". Colm was survived by his wife Victoria, and his three children Victoria, Amy and Colm Jnr.

Trail 6 – Sports

This trail is sponsored by Geraldine and Gerry McCollum, huge Manchester United fans who I was privileged to show around George Best's childhood home last year, so it is appropriate that they are sponsoring this section - in memory of their son Christopher, who features in my 2020 book - which features Roselawn's most famous resident.

This Sports trail features a number of graves featured on my football-themed tour of the cemetery, as well as those proficient in a range of other sports.

Norman Mawhinney - U-1618 – Go kart and motorbike racing - this headstone commemorates 'Our beloved son and our dear brother Norman died as the result of a car accident 24th November 1967 aged 20 years', whilst registered as living at 123 Saintfield Road, Belfast. The headstone contains the image of a go kart above the words 'Champion 1967'. Also commemorated on this headstone is 'His dear brother Joe who died 19th May 1992' aged 76 whilst living at 66 Glenholme Drive, Belfast, with the image of a motorbike beside his inscription.

Arthur John Bell - T-1869 - motorcycling - born in 1915, 'Artie' Bell was one of the most dominant motorcycle road racers in the period following the Second World War. After winning the Isle of Man Senior Tourist Trophy race in 1948, Bell went on to win the Junior TT in 1950, and also triumphed in the Dutch TT and Swiss Grand Prix. Bell owned a garage and workshop on Belfast's Cregagh Road, and was registered as living at Stonefield, Boardmills, Lisburn when he died on 7 August 1972 aged 57.

James Reid - T-2062 - football - Reid died on 14 December 1972 aged 86 whilst living at 2 Myrtle Street, Belfast. Reid was part of the Glentoran team who won the 1914 Vienna Cup, the first British Club to win a European trophy. As Irish Cup Winners, Glentoran were invited to partake in the Vienna Cup alongside Burnley and Glasgow Celtic who were FA Cup and Scottish Cup winners respectively. The British sides were joined by Hertha Berlin, representatives from Bratislava and Prague, and a Viennese Select XI. The Glens were a team mostly made up of shipyard workers, and set sail for Europe from Larne Harbour on 18 May 1914 for their arduous journey across Europe. The highlights of this adventure for Glentoran were a 4-1 victory over Hertha Berlin, and 5-0 win over the Viennese Select XI, the latter result sealing the Vienna Cup. The amazing story of this Glentoran team is told in the '*One Saturday Before The War*' book by my good friend Sam Robinson.

Richard Alan Craig - S-811 - cricket, shooting and rugby - 'in sweet memory of our dear son Richard Alan Craig died 3rd September 1976, aged 19 years' whilst living at 28 Thornhill Drive, Belfast. Amongst images featured at the top of the headstone is a cricket bat and ball, birds and a smoking gun, and a rugby ball, a set of posts and boots suggesting that Craig was a keen sports fan. The base of the grave states 'He is not dead the child of our affection, But gone into that school, Where he no longer needs our fond protection, And Christ himself doth rule'.

William Irvine - V-1526 - hockey and cricket - William, known as Billy, was on a trip with friends to watch a test match between the West Indies and England when he was found dead in a swimming pool in Barbados. A former member of the East Antrim hockey club, Irvine had also played cricket for Cliftonville cricket club before retiring due to a persistent back injury. Amongst numerous death notices in the *Belfast Telegraph* were a couple from his colleagues in Gallahers. This headstone contains a hockey symbol, with Irvine registered as living at 255 Tennent Street, Belfast when he died on 7 March 1981 (the same day as the McElhinney family featured in the following entry) aged 29.

Also interred in this plot is Billy's father, William Irvine senior, who was living at 5 Charleville Street, Belfast when he died on 1 May 1991 aged 71.

McElhinney - V-1577 - rugby - 'in loving memory of Robert S. (Bertie) [41], his wife Patricia I [38] and their children Eleanor Ruth [14] and Carol Patricia [10] died 7th March 1981 as a result of an accident'. The McElhinney family, who lived at 70 Knockeden Park, Belfast, were driving to Dublin where Bertie was to watch Ireland play England at Lansdowne Road whilst his wife and children went shopping. The family's Citroen car was in collision with a CIE bus at Balbriggan, causing both vehicles to be engulfed in flames. Bertie was employed by the Department of Agriculture, and was Chairman and Past President of the Civil Service Rugby Club and an Ulster junior selector, with death notices including from the Civil Service Bowling, Cricket, Lawn Tennis and Ladies Committee of the Rugby Club.

Tommy Givan - V-1474 - cycling - a stalwart of local track cycling, Givan competed for the Maryland Wheelers, and was a former National Track Champion. After his death on 15 September 1981 aged 62 whilst living at 26 Orby Parade, the velodrome at Orangefield was renamed the Tommy Givan Track in his honour, and a memorial stone to him stands at the entrance to the track. The track is a 396-metre outdoor banked oval track surfaced in tarmac, opened for competition in 1957 when track cycling enjoyed tremendous support, and is the only surviving facility of this kind in Ulster. The annual Tommy Givan Memorial road race, promoted by Maryland Wheelers, still continues to this day.

Aaron Currie, MBE - T-3687 - swimming - Currie is still remembered fondly in East Belfast from his time working with his brother Tommy (buried at plot T-683) in Templemore Avenue baths, teaching many local children how to swim, and for which he was awarded the MBE in 1970. Templemore Avenue baths opened in the late 1800s, and are currently undergoing a huge renovation funded by the National Lottery. Currie is also commemorated at Aaron House, named in his honour, with the house part of the Ballybeen community since it opened in 1995. Now managed by the Presbyterian Church, Aaron House accommodates 14 residents on a permanent basis, with a day care centre supporting nine people, with two additional rooms available for respite care. Aaron Currie, remembered on the headstone as a 'devoted husband and father', was living at 167 Clarawood Park, Belfast when he died on 18 June 1982 aged 76, with his wife Catherine (Kitty), 'a dearly loved wife and mother called home 8th February 1993' aged 86 whilst living at Belmont Clinic, 81 Tillyburn Park, Belfast.

Joe Bambrick - S-3027 - football - born on 3 November 1905, Bambrick played football for Chelsea, Walsall, Glentoran and, most notably, Linfield. A former gas worker, he was a prolific goalscorer in the Irish League and the Football League, adept at getting into good scoring positions and athletic enough to make the final touch count. 'Head, heel or toe, slip it to Joe' became a famous catchphrase when referring to Bambrick, and this phrase is replicated on his headstone. Joe's six goals for Ireland against Wales at Celtic Park, Belfast on 1 February 1930 in a 7-0 win still remains the record score for a British Isles player in an international fixture. Joe was living at 219 Roden Street, Belfast, the location of an Ulster History Circle blue plaque in his memory, when he died on 13 October 1983 aged 77.

William (Billy) Seeds - S-841 - snooker - commemorated on a plaque at this grave, featuring the image of snooker balls, is Billy Seeds 'N. Ireland snooker champion 1954' who was living at 42 Tyndale Park, Belfast when he died on 23 April 1987 aged 63. Also mentioned on the panel is John (Jack) Seeds, commemorated as having served with the '121st Royal Engineers 36th Ulster Division'. Jack was living at 42 Tyndale Park when he died on 16 October 1976 aged 83. Also commemorated on the panel is 'Isobel (Lizzie) Best 09-11-1946~10-06-2005'.

Mervyn Edwin Cotter - R-2217 - body-building - Cotter was born and raised in east Belfast, and was educated at Mountpottinger School, then working for Harland and Wolff as a boiler-maker. In his spare time he trained to tone his muscular frame for body-building competitions, in 1952 lifting three titles - Mr Northern Ireland, Mr Great Britain 'Health and Strength', and the prestigious Mr Universe. A story was also told of how his trademark was to lift his Norton motorbike above his head. Cotter married his wife Geraldine in 1957 and was survived by her and their three children and six grandchildren when he died on 14 May 1998 aged 70, whilst living at 3 Knock Way, Belfast.

John Alexander Henning, MBE - S-4169 - athletics - 'Born 25th September 1910 died 27 November 1999' aged 89 whilst living at 15 Battenberg Street, Belfast, with the headstone also commemorating John's 'Dear wife Sarah (Sadie) born 12th June 1913 Died 30th March 1984'. Henning spent almost all of his life on Belfast's Shankill Road, an area that he described as 'The Heart of the Empire'. One of a family of six, incredibly John spent only four years at school (Jersey Street Primary) before starting work soon after his tenth birthday as a paperboy selling the Belfast Telegraph. In 1929, John joined Ulsterville Harriers and, in the mid 1930s, was selected to run in three international cross-country races, before losing interest and retiring aged 26. After the Second World War, John joined Duncairn Nomads and resumed training this time as a marathon runner. John won the 1946 NI Marathon Championship, retaining his title for the next ten years, also winning the 1947 Manchester Marathon, 1948 Sheffield Marathon and the 1948 Liverpool Centenary Marathon. At the age of 48, John was selected for the 1958 Empire Games marathon in Cardiff, possibly becoming the oldest ever runner in a major games, finishing 20th in the race. John then set himself a series of challenges including to run to every Irish League football ground to watch his beloved Linfield, leaving for the remaining trek to Derry City at 4:00am. In

1960, to celebrate his 50th birthday, John ran from Dublin to Belfast completing the 108 miles in 16 hours and 20 minutes. Henning then won World Veteran Championship medals in Toronto 1975, Hanover 1977, Gothenburg 1979 and Christchurch 1981, running 100 laps around Windsor Park at the age of 60. John's running career sadly came to an end in the 1990s due to injuries received when he was hit by a car. Just a few years before he died, John whispered to a friend -'I'm well over 80 but still acting like a wee lad - it's been a great life'.

Thomas Maginnes - P-2824 - bowls - 'in loving memory of a devoted husband, father and grandfather Thomas (Tommy) died 14th September 2002' aged 51 whilst living at 57 Sydney Street West, Belfast. This headstone contains a photo of Maginnes and an image of a bowler with the words 'N.B.W.M.C Bowling Section'. N.B.W.M.C (North Belfast Working Men's Club) at 32 Danube Street, Belfast was founded in 1894 by linen merchants wishing to provide a venue for constructive social, sporting and educational outlets for mill workers, and houses a bar, dance/events hall, bowling and billiards clubs, and is still active in 2021.

George Best - S-295 - football - born on 22 May 1946, George is regarded as one of the greatest footballers of all time. Spending most of his club career at Manchester United where he won the European Cup, he was named European Footballer of the Year in 1968. Best was also capped 37 times for Northern Ireland between 1964 and 1977. With his good looks and playboy lifestyle, Best became one of the first media celebrity footballers, earning the nickname 'El Beatle' in 1966, but his extravagant lifestyle led to personal problems, most notably alcoholism, from which he suffered for the rest of his life. Best said of his career: 'I spent a lot of money on

booze, birds [women] and fast cars – the rest I just squandered'. After football, Best spent some time as a football analyst, received a liver transplant in 2002 and died on 25 November 2005 aged 59. George was predeceased by his mother, Annie Mary Best, who died on 12 October 1978 aged 56, with his father Richard (Dickie) dying on 16 April 2008 aged 88, both whilst registered as living at 16 Burren Way, Belfast. For the last few years I have looked after 16 Burren Way with EastSide Partnership through Airbnb, meeting many great people, including Sir Michael Parkinson and the McCollums as mentioned at the start of this chapter, during that time.

Hugh Liddy - W-506 - GAA - Liddy was living at 32 Brookvale Avenue, Belfast when he died on 11 December 2006 aged 36, with an ornamental ball with the words 'O'Neills All Ireland' resting on his grave, along with a number of other religious objects. Another GAA follower buried in Roselawn - Y-1569 - is Brendan Laverty recorded on his headstone as 'A devoted father, loving grandfather and dear partner 19th Feb 1956 - 7th Feb 2018' with the base of the headstone stating 'I'll not keep you I know your [sic] busy'. The headstone, which includes the representation of a Celtic cross, also features an image of Laverty and the Antrim county logo, suggesting that he was a follower of Gaelic games in the county.

William (Billy) Mahood - W-1545 - kick boxing - the left-hand side of this headstone contains the image of a clock, above the words 'the hands of time stand still', with the main section of the headstone commemorating 'a loving husband and dad [who] died suddenly 31st July 2011 aged 44 years', with the base of the headstone stating 'gone from our lives but never from our hearts'. A photo of Mahood and a Pro Kick logo adorns William's headstone suggesting that William, who was living at 3 Lyndhurst View Road, Belfast when he died, was a keen participant of this increasingly popular sport.

Hugh Albert Swain - W-2260 - weightlifting - 'beloved husband, father and grandfather passed away 7th Oct 2012 aged 47, with the base of the headstone stating 'In our hearts forever xxxx', with plaques at the bottom of the headstone remembering a 'Special husband. If tears could build a stairway and memories a lane, I would walk right up to heaven and bring you home again' and a 'Special Dad. Precious thoughts of times together. Happy memories will last forever'. As well as an image of Swain, the headstone contains an image of a weightlifter. A similar image appears on a headstone at Y-7 commemorating Neal (Neo) Auld 'Passed away 22nd August 2015 aged 36 years' with a photo of Auld also on the headstone, and a plaque at the bottom of the headstone stating 'Shine bright like a diamond'.

Paul Nicholls - Y-2112 - golf - this headstone commemorates 'a beloved husband, devoted dad, grandad, stepdad and pops 02/07/1948 - 11/09/2016 Sadly missed by friends & family'. The bottom of the headstone is the representation of a flag and reads 'Golf - a day spent in a round of strenuous idleness (Wordsworth)'. At the bottom of the headstone is a flag with the word Kernow below it. The flag would appear to be Saint Piran's Flag, the flag of Cornwall, apparently often used by Cornish people as a symbol of their identity.

George Matchett - Y-2161 - football - 'devoted and loving husband, father and grandfather died 25th May 2018 aged 69 years', with the base of this headstone stating 'Safe in God's keeping'. George was captain of Carrick Rangers when the club performed one of the greatest local giant-killing acts defeating Linfield 2-1 in the Irish Cup Final at The Oval in 1976, with Gary Prenter scoring both goals. George, the first of the team to die, was a true gentleman who often chatted to my Dad, and occasionally to me too, when we were responsible for cutting the grass at the church George attended, Knocknagoney Church of Ireland.

Sammy Pavis - Y-2248 - snooker and football - born in Ballymacarrett, East Belfast, Pavis signed for Glentoran in the early 1960s, scoring 54 goals in 74 games and winning an Irish League medal. After a disagreement with the club's then manager Gibby MacKenzie, Pavis was snapped up by Linfield. In 260 games for the Blues he scored 237 goals in five seasons. In 1967/68 he was fourth in the European 'Golden Boot' award, behind the great Eusebio of Benfica. The straight-talking, wise-cracking Pavis, who was also the Northern Ireland snooker champion for a time after he retired from football, was affectionately known to the Linfield legions as 'Sammy Save Us', with the fans invariably looking to him for vital goals. Pavis died on 4 July 2019, and his headstone remembers 'a dearly loved husband and father' and contains the Linfield FC logo with the word 'Legend' below, as well as a snooker table with the words 'N.I & All Ireland Champion'.

Tommy Breslin - S-3216 - football - a former Cliftonville player of some note, Breslin died on 27 August 2019 aged 58 whilst on holiday in Spain. Breslin was assistant to Eddie Patterson from 2005 and took the reins himself at Solitude in 2011, leading Cliftonville to back-to-back league titles in the 2012/13 and 2013/14 seasons. In four-and-a-half years, he won eight trophies, making him the most successful boss in the north Belfast club's 140-year history. As well as the Gibson Cup twice, he guided the club to three consecutive League Cup triumphs, two County Antrim Shield victories and a Charity Shield win. Also interred in this plot is Tommy's mother Mary Philomena Breslin who died on 30 October 1980 aged 53, whilst his father Thomas Jude Breslin died on 30 May 1998 aged 70, both whilst living at 53 Brookvale Street, Belfast.

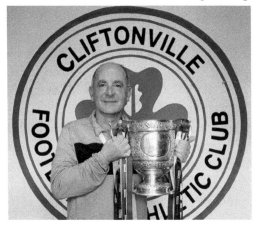

Trail 7 – Football Clubs

This trail is sponsored by William Kingsberry, a long-suffering friend of mine, who has also sponsored my previous books, only agreeing to sponsor this trail if I featured Leeds and the Glens!

Trail 7 profiles 21 headstones that feature the logos of football clubs. As well as the usual suspects, I've tried to include a few of the lesser-known clubs, and a few local teams, but sadly, I've yet to spot a reference to Ards or Norwich on any headstone.

Albert Boal McKibbin - V-1201 - Arsenal - 'my beloved husband and devoted father ... died 5th January 1982' aged 73, whilst living at 82 Mayo Street, Belfast. This headstone contains both the Arsenal crest and a Gunner symbol. Also buried in this grave is 'his loving wife' Emily McKibbin who was living at Tennent Street Care Home, 1 Tennent Street, Belfast when she died on 3 December 2005 aged 93.

Samuel Scott - V-2571 - Harland & Wolff Welders, 1st Liverpool and Cliftonville - 'In loving memory of Samuel a beloved husband and father died 23rd July 1991', with a plaque at the bottom of this headstone placed 'In remembrance of Scottie from his friends at H & W Welders FC, 1st Liverpool FC, Cliftonville FC'.

Hugh McGuinness - R-632 - Crumlin Star - a 'dear husband and our devoted father', McGuinness was living at 14 Elmfield Street, Ardoyne, Belfast when he died on 3 June 1992 aged 63. A Crumlin Star logo features on his headstone. Crumlin Star Football Club is an intermediate association club based in Belfast, and playing in the Premier Division of the Northern Amateur Football League. Also interred in this grave is McGuinness's grandson Kevin McGuinness who was living at 23 Estoril Park, Belfast when he died on 30 March 1985 aged 2 weeks.

Robert James Corkhill - P-1677 - Liverpool, Rangers and Glentoran - Corkhill died on 10 April 1997 aged 52 whilst living at 61 Pims Avenue,

Belfast. As well as the Liverpool and Glentoran crests, this headstone also contains the logo of the Sandy Row Rangers Supporters Club. The base of this headstone states 'If love could have saved you, you would have lived forever'. Also buried in this grave, and commemorated on a plaque with the image of a teddy bear, is 'Baby Keva', a stillborn female baby of Joanne Corkhill, registered as living at 33 Orangefield Gardens, Belfast at the time of her death on 25 September 2003.

Alfred Frederick Watson - P-1890 - Glentoran - 'A dear husband, Devoted father and grandfather died 27th May 1998' aged 66, whilst living at 1 Carncaver Road, Castlereagh, with the logo of the Glentoran Castlereagh Supporters Club featuring on this headstone. Also commemorated on the headstone is 'Edith Watson A dear wife Devoted mother and grandmother 30th October 2004 aged 79'. The headstone also features a rose, and a photo of each of the couple, with the base of the headstone stating 'Peacefully sleeping Till we meet again'.

Martin McLaughlin - P-1927 - Celtic - 'treasured memories of our only son and brother Martin (Biggs) Died 6th June 1998 aged 15', whilst living at 4 Seaforde Gardens, Short Strand, Belfast. A photo of McLaughlin features on this headstone, along with the Celtic logo and the words 'You'll Never Walk Alone', with the base of the headstone stating 'A beautiful life, too soon to end, you died as you lived, everyone's friend'. A plaque at the foot of this headstone includes another photo of McLaughlin along with the words 'Low lie the fields of Athenry, Where once we watched the small freebird fly, Our love was on the wing, We had dreams and songs to sing, It's so lonely round the Fields of Athenry. Oh baby let the freebird fly'.

Courban - P-692 - Tottenham Hotspur - this fine, black double headstone commemorates 'Jordan, A dearly loved son and brother Born 21st April 1982 Died 24th November 1998' aged 16, and 'Dean a very special son and brother Born 23rd October 1978 Died 16th February 1997' aged 18. Dean was buried on 24 February 1997, with 'Dedicated Tissue' (implying that Dean was a transplant donor) also being buried in this grave on 2 June 2005. Both brothers were living at 103 Clonduff Drive, Belfast at the time of their deaths. A plaque with the Spurs badge is at the base of this headstone stating 'A golden heart stopped beating two smiling eyes at rest God broke our hearts to prove to us He only takes the best. Mum, Dad, Brandon and Jordan'. This would seem to suggest that Dean, at least, was a Spurs fan. Also commemorated on another plaque at this grave is Lou (Elizabeth Nancy) Carson who was living at 1b Sheskin Way, Cregagh, Belfast when she died on 19 May 2005 aged 83.

Steven Colwell - W-582 - Chelsea - 'a much loved Son, Daddy, Brother and Uncle Steven Craig (Stevie) Murdered by P.S.N.I. 16th April 2006 aged 23 years', with the headstone featuring a Chelsea logo, and the base stating 'Gone from our lives but never from our hearts'. Colwell, of 16 Forthriver Link, Belfast, died after police fired on a car he was driving which failed to stop at a checkpoint in Ballynahinch. Colwell had been driving the stolen silver BMW when he encountered the police checkpoint. When an officer approached the vehicle, it was claimed that Mr Colwell attempted to drive away but was blocked by other cars. Another officer (known as Officer O) claimed the car was then driven straight towards him when he fired two shots.

Thomas McDonagh - W-786 - Nottingham Forest - 'in loving memory of a beloved Son, Dad and Brother Thomas Paul (Tucker) died 30th March 2007 aged 36 years' whilst registered as living at 12 Walnut Court, Belfast. As well as a photo of 'Tucker', this headstone contains the Nottingham Forest logo which incorporates two stars commemorating Forest's European Cup victories in 1979 and 1980.

David Proctor - W-1936 - Shankill Junior Football Club - 'Precious memories of David beloved partner of Julie devoted Dad of Joshua and Ethan died 9th September 2010 aged 38' whilst living at 82 Glencairn Street, Belfast. The bottom of the headstone states 'Mizpah the Lord watch between me and thee while we are absent one from another'.

A football-shaped plaque with a Shankill Junior Football Club logo 'Est.1987' is at the base of the grave, along with the words 'Davy the butcher's green and white army', suggesting that Proctor worked as a butcher and was a big fan of Northern Ireland.

Alexander James Thompson - W-1435 - West Ham - 'much loved partner, father and grandfather died 11th January 2011' aged 45 whilst living at 27 Blythe Street, Belfast. As well as a photo of Alex, the Hammers' striking logo adorns this headstone, with the base of the headstone stating 'Gone from our home but not from our hearts'. Around Remembrance Day a fine wreath, in the claret and blue of the Hammers, is placed at this plot.

James Donaldson - W-2107 - Portadown - 'a beloved partner, step-father and grandfather died 20th March 2012 aged 76 years' with the base of the grave stating 'Forever in our hearts'. The Portadown F.C. logo features on the headstone, whilst a plaque at the bottom of the headstone states 'There are no goodbyes for us wherever you are, you will always be in our hearts xxx The Lord is my shepherd'.

Gary Quinn - W-2183 - Everton - '(Quinner) in loving memory of Gary, devoted partner of Mary, father and grandfather died 13.10.2012 aged 52 years' with the base of the headstone stating 'Gone from our home'. The headstone also features a photo of Quinn wearing an Everton kit and an image of a footballer, with the Everton club crest featuring at the base of the plot.

Stirling - W-2362 - Northern Ireland - 'Ryan Craig (Incey) 1.8.1987 - 16.1.2013 A much loved son, brother and dad', with an image of 'Incey' and the logos of both Northern Ireland and Manchester United featuring on the headstone. The base of the headstone states 'Forever in our thoughts. Always in our hearts' with a plaque on the grave featuring a photo of a smiling father and son with the words 'Love You Dad x'.

On occasions, there are also a couple of bottles of Corrs placed on the grave.

George Heenan - W-2421 - Harland & Wolff Welders FC - this headstone reads 'precious memories of George (Hugh Alexander) a much loved husband, father and grandfather died 22nd April 2013 aged 59 years', with the striking Harland & Wolff Welders FSC (Football Social Club) logo at the top of the headstone. Plaques at this plot also are 'in loving memory of my dear husband George My Love, my life, my soulmate from your darling wife Jacquie xx' and 'in loving memory of our Daddy George. The tears in our eyes we can wipe away The ache in our hearts will always stay. Loved always Leanne and Georgia'.

John (John Boy) Hill - W-2663 - Blackburn and Barcelona - this headstone commemorates a 'much loved son, brother and daddy Born 10/07/1983 - Died 05/04/2014', with the logos of both Blackburn and Barcelona featuring on the headstone. The base of the headstone states 'Forever in our hearts we will always love you', with a plaque at the bottom of the grave stating 'Daddy we love you. Today, tomorrow, Always, Evie & Scarlett'.

Mat Goddard - W-3141 - Queens Park Rangers - 'in loving memory of Mat Goddard much loved son, brother and friend to many 23.3.1973 - 24.12.2014', with the base of the headstone stating 'never more than a thought away loved and remembered every day'. The headstone contains a photo of Goddard, as well as the Queens Park Rangers logo.

Grzegorz Lozynski - Y-1450 - Górnik Zabrze and Real Madrid - 'with love we remember Grzegorz born 5th January 1981 Died 4th December 2016 Zawsze bedziemy cie kochac', with the latter translating from Polish to 'we will always love you'. The headstone contains the logos of both Real Madrid and Górnik Zabrze. Górnik Zabrze is one of the most successful Polish football clubs in history, winning the most Polish Championship titles, together with Ruch Chorzów. The club was a dominant force in the 1960s and 1980s, and holds the record for

winning the most consecutive Polish Championship titles (5) and Polish Cup titles (5). In addition, the club was 1969–70 Cup Winners' Cup runners-up. A Górnik flag and a scarf are also on Lozynski's grave on occasions.

Leonard Tarr - Y-40 - Leeds United and Barcelona - this headstone commemorates 'our beloved son and brother died 16th October 2017 aged 36' and contains the logos of both Leeds United and Barcelona. A plaque at the base of the grave states 'May the winds of Heaven blow softly and whisper in your ear how much we love and miss you and wish that you were here'.

Alfred James (Jim) Harbinson - Y-2210 - Manchester United – this headstone which states 'M.U.F.C.' at the top - above the name Harbinson - is 'in loving memory of a beloved husband, father, grandfather and brother died 29th July 2018 aged 54 years', with 'forever in our hearts' at the base of the headstone, and a Manchester United crest and a photo of Jim also on the headstone. A plaque, also containing two Manchester United crests, on the grave states 'In loving memory of my dear Dad From your loving son Ryan. Time goes by without you days turn in to years, each moment holds a memory and many silent tears'. Also on occasions there are two Manchester United mugs on this grave. I think it's a fairly safe bet that Jim would have been supporting the team in red during the Manchester derby.

Bertie McMinn - Y-1794 - Distillery and Shankill United - this headstone commemorates 'a beloved husband, father, granda and great-granda Bertie Died 4th October 2018' aged 60, with the base of the headstone featuring the club crests of both Distillery and Shankill United. One of the most gifted players of his generation, McMinn is best remembered as one of the great entertainers and goalscorers of the Irish League, most notably with Distillery, signing for the Whites three times, and always gravitating back to the side he considered his football spiritual home. McMinn once said: 'What I loved about Distillery was the supporters. It didn't matter why you had a bad game, there was always next week, that was their attitude. They were great people'. McMinn also played for and managed Ards F.C, and was also a former assistant manager and committee member of Shankill United in the Premier Division of the Amateur League.

Trail 8 – World Wars

This trail is sponsored by Alistair McCartney, an Organ Builder & Historiographer, who has also supported, and contributed to, my previous books, with a family friend Sergeant Cecil McKenna featuring in this section.

Trail 8 features those who served in the World Wars, and I am especially indebted to my learned friend Nigel Henderson for his help with this trail.

David Lyness - D-607 - 'C.S.M. 2nd R.U.R. killed in France 15th Sept. 1914'. Born on 26 April 1880 in Charles Street, Lurgan, Lyness married Helena Collins at North Strand Church of Ireland, Dublin on 12 April 1904, and was living at 158 New Lodge Road, Belfast when he enlisted. Company Sergeant Major David Andrew Lyness was serving with 2nd Battalion, Royal Irish Rifles when he was killed in action on 15 September 1914 aged 34, and is commemorated on the La Ferte-sous-Jouarre Memorial in France. Buried in this grave is Helena Lyness who died on 30 November 1958 aged 78, and William Lyness who died on 30 September 1974 aged 70, both whilst living at 24 Manor Street, Belfast, and Maude Lyness who died at the Lansdowne Clinic, Belfast on 19 December 1992 aged 87.

Alfred Harry Nugent - C-1474 - a simple plaque at the base of this headstone commemorates Rifleman Alfred Harry Nugent who died '9th October 1916 In Flanders Fields'. Nugent was born in 1891 at Camberwell to Harry Nugent and Emma Nugent (née Morgan), later of Sylvester Road East, Dulwich, London, and was serving with the 1st/9th Battalion (Queen Victoria's Rifles), London Regiment when he was killed in action aged 25, and is commemorated on the Thiepval Memorial, France. Buried in this grave is Richard Redvers Lester who died on 26 January 1965 aged 65, Edith M Lester who died on 16 February 1971 aged 72, and Elizabeth Nugent who died on 9 April 1978 aged 72, all three living at 37 Whitehall Parade, Belfast at the time of their deaths.

Samuel Richard Burnside - S-1382 - 'Killed in action in Belgium 25 October 1917'. Born on 1 June 1882 in West Derby, Lancashire to John Burnside and Rebecca Burnside (née Rutledge) later of county Monaghan, Burnside married Margaret Eleanor Johnston on 27 April 1910 at Christ Church, Belfast. Private Burnside was serving with 108th Army Field Artillery Brigade, Army Service Corps, when he died when a brick wall collapsed on a hut on 25 October 1917. Burnside is  buried in Poperinghe New Military Cemetery, Belgium, with his address at the time of his death, aged 35, registered as 270 Cupar Street, Belfast. Buried in this grave is Samuel's wife Margaret Eleanor Burnside who was living at 1 Cherry Lane, Lisburn when she died on 18 November 1975 aged 90, and their son 'Samuel Richardson Burnside 1914 – 2004', who would have been aged 3 when his father was killed.

Captain John McMinn - U-2362 - commemorated on this headstone is 'Capt John McMinn Killed in action 27th May 1918'. Born on 1 June 1883 at Walton Street, Belfast to Robert McMinn and Margaret McMinn (née Brown), later of 4 Southport Street, Belfast, Captain McMinn married Isabella Kirkwood on 8 May 1907 at Falls Road Methodist Church, Belfast, then living at 16 Crumlin Gardens, Belfast. Captain McMinn was serving with the 14th Battalion, Royal Irish Rifles (attached to the 5th Battalion, Durham Light Infantry) when he was killed aged 35, and is commemorated on the Soissons Memorial in France. Interred in this plot is Captain McMinn's wife Isabella who was living at 16 Crumlin Gardens, Belfast when she died on 24 January 1969 aged 83.

Archie Maginnes - R-1190 - 'R.N. Lost at sea 1940 in the war'. Ordinary Seaman Maginnes, P/JX 189416, was lost on HMS Acheron, a British Navy Destroyer which hit a mine and sank off the Isle of Wight on 17 December 1940 with the loss of 151 crew on board, including Maginnes. The son of Archibald and Sarah Ann Maginnes, and husband of Margaret Maginnes, of Belfast, Maginnes was 33 at the time of his death and is commemorated on the Portsmouth Naval Memorial. His wife Margaret was living at 12 Knockeden Parade, Belfast when she died in 23 March 1985 aged 74, with their son Archibald Maginnes dying on 2 February 1996 aged 58, whilst also living at 12 Knockeden Parade.

James Lynas - R-588 - 'Born 5th November 1902 Killed in action RN [Royal Navy] 17th January 1942'. Able Seaman Lynas was onboard *HMS Matabele* in January 1942 when she formed the screen for the cruiser *Trinidad* on Convoy PQ 8 from Iceland to Murmansk. The convoy of eight merchant ships plus escorts departed on 11 January, and came under torpedo attack on 17 January by German submarine *U-454* under the command of Kapitänleutnant Burkhard Hackländer. At 10.21pm *U-454* fired and hit the *Matabele* in the stern area with a single torpedo which detonated a magazine, causing the destroyer to sink in less than two minutes, leading to the loss of 198 lives including Able Seaman Lynas. There were only two survivors. The only interment in this grave is James's wife Mary Lynas 'Born 7th February 1897 Died 30 April 1986' whilst living at 11 Beechill Park South, Belfast.

James Lockhart - T-3066 - a plaque at the base of this headstone is 'In loving memory of our dear father Sgt. James Lockhart R.U.R. Died

Active Service 26.3.42 Interred City Cemetery'. Lockhart died at the Military Hospital, Hatfield, Hertfordshire aged 37, with a home address of 6 Hunter Street, Belfast and is buried at Plot L-307 in the Glenalina extension of Belfast City Cemetery. Buried in this grave is 'a dear husband & beloved father' William Smith who was living at 95 Donegall Road, Belfast when he died on 21 June 1973 aged 73, and 'his wife and a much loved mother and nanny Henrietta' Smith who was living at 6 Felt Street, Belfast when she died on 24 August 1997 aged 86.

Sergeant Thomas J. Whiteside - T-3077 - 'R.A.F. killed in action May 1942 interred in British War Cemetery Haverlee Belgium'. Buried in this grave is Thomas's father James Neill Whiteside who died on 7 April 1973 aged 82 whilst living at 64 Dee Street, Belfast, James Adams Whiteside who was living at 24 Ardcarn Drive, Dundonald when he died on 11 December 1980 aged 64, and Sarah Whiteside who was also living at 64 Dee Street when she died on 4 May 1981 aged 87, but the latter two interments are, sadly, not recorded on the headstone.

William Arthur Robinson - E-161 - 'Sergt/Observer R.A.F. Missing on active service 10th June 1943' aged 22. Robinson was lost on aircraft Lancaster EE113 whilst serving in 619 Squadron, and is commemorated on Panel 163 at the Runnymede Memorial in Surrey. Buried in this plot is Joseph Norman Robinson who died on 26 September 1960 aged 66, and Barbara E Robinson who died on 16 November 1969 aged 73, both whilst living at 7 Thirlmere Gardens, Belfast although the latter is not commemorated on the headstone.

Sergeant Charles Cecil McKenna - T-724 - 'Sgt Airgunner killed in action 12th April 1944'. Sergeant McKenna was serving with the Royal Air Force Volunteer Reserve on board Avro Lancaster ME752 with RAF 50 Squadron. McKenna was an Air Gunner on the bomber which took off at 20.54 on 11 April 1944 from RAF Skellingthorpe, Lincolnshire and disappeared without trace. McKenna was born at 1 Lismore Villa, Newtownbreda and lived all his life there, with section sponsor Alastair McCartney's father evacuated to live there during the war. As well as being commemorated on this headstone, Sergeant McKenna's name is on Panel 233 of the Runnymede Memorial, Surrey, and the Roll of Honour in Knockbreda Parish Church, Belfast. Buried in this grave is Charles' father Charles K McKenna who died on 23 February 1971 aged 80, and his mother Janet McKenna who died on 30 June 1975 aged 75, both whilst registered as living at 69 Richardson Street, Belfast.

James McNair - U-2105 - a plaque at the base of this headstone remembers 'James McNair Lost at sea Aged 22, in the sinking of *H.M.S. Mourne* 15th June 1944'. After commissioning in April 1943, *HMS Mourne* served on convoy escort missions and participated in anti-submarine warfare exercises off Lough Foyle and Larne. Following the Normandy landings of Operation Overlord, *Mourne* was deployed to the western entrance of the English Channel as a screening operation, serving as part of the 5th Escort Group. At 13:45 on 15 June 1944, the bow of *Mourne* was hit by a torpedo fired by German submarine *U-767*, causing an ignition in the ship magazine. The ship was sunk with the loss of 111 lives, including James, with only 27 survivors. Buried in this grave is James' mother Mary Ellen McNair who died on 20 April 1968 aged 70, and his father James senior who died on 3 June 1980 aged 83, both whilst living at 140 Rosebery Road, Belfast. Also commemorated on the headstone is another son 'Robert died 23rd March 2014 aged 89', with the plaque at the grave 'Also remembering Robert's wife Ruth McNair Resting in Dundonald'.

George McKnight - E-381 - 'RAF killed in action 26 June 1944 buried in Budapest'. Sergeant McKnight aged 23, a Wireless Operator with 142 Squadron, was on board a Wellington BX LN748 which crashed in Hungary killing all four crew on board including McKnight, with the four buried in Budapest War Cemetery. Buried in this grave is Thomas McKnight who died on 4 August 1961 aged 65, and Mary A. McKnight who died on 24 April 1975 aged 80, both whilst living at 30 Cosgrave

Street, Belfast, and Thomas McKnight who was living at 15 York Park, Belfast when he died on 28 January 1979 aged 56.

William James Moffatt - C-2320 - 'killed in action 10th July 1944 Interred in France'. Born in Belfast in 1908, in 1911 Moffatt was living at 21 Woodlee Street, Belfast. Moffatt was a Warrant Officer Class II (C.S.M.), with the 1st Battalion, Highland Light Infantry (City of Glasgow Regiment) when he died at Cheux, Caen, Normandy, and was buried in the St Manvieu War Cemetery. Buried in this grave is Rose Quee who was living at 7 Lackagh Street, Belfast when she died on 15 May 1965 aged 72, Charles Quee of 39 Thistle Street, Belfast who died on 1 September 1979 aged 85, and Georgina Moffatt of 97 Beechfield Street, Belfast who died on 28 April 2006 aged 91.

Frederick McLernon - C-1317 - 'killed in action in Italy 12th December 1944'. Born on 4 November 1912, McLernon's father Francis owned a grocer's shop in Magherafelt. Lance Corporal McLernon served with the Royal Ulster Rifles, and was attached to the 2nd Battalion of the London Irish Rifles when he died on 12 December 1944 aged 32, and was buried at Santerno Valley War Cemetery, Italy, with the personal inscription on his headstone reading 'Faithful Unto Death' Remembered Always By His Loving Wife, Son And Mother'. Buried in this plot is Elizabeth Parker who was living at 50 Moatview Park, Dundonald when she died on 26 December 1962 aged 70, Robert Busby Parker who died on 11 May 1966 aged 73 whilst living at 7 Ardcloon Park, Rathcoole, Frederick's wife Jean McLernon who died on 31 July 1967 aged 49 whilst also living at 7 Ardcloon Park, and Evelyn Leckey who was living at 32 Combe Bank, Brixham, Devon when she died on 2 August 1997 aged 78.

Thomas Norman Dunlop - C-654 - 'R.A.F V.R. killed in action 8th March 1945'. Dunlop was aged 19 and serving with Unit 57 Squadron when his Lancaster I PB852 took off from East Kirkby airfield on 7 March 1945 with six crew onboard to bomb oil installations, with the plane disappearing without trace. Dunlop is also commemorated on the Runnymede Memorial in Surrey. Buried in this grave is Dunlop's father William Dunlop who died on 20 August 1962 aged 79, and his mother Margaret Dunlop who died on 29 October 1965 aged 78, both whilst living at 69 Donovan Parade, Belfast.

Robert Small Beastall - D-240 - Beastall was living at 15 Parkgate Avenue, Belfast when he died on 14 February 1959 aged 59, with his wife Jean Beastall living at 75 Church Road, Holywood when she died on 26 July 1988 aged 89. Robert was a brother of Rifleman John Beastall who, according to his memorial on the family headstone in Dundonald Cemetery - E4-655 - was serving with '10th (Service) Battalion (South Belfast Volunteers), Royal Irish Rifles. [when he was] Accidentally killed, 25 June 1917, aged 22 years'. John and Robert were sons of William and Marian Beastall who lived in 15 Parkgate Avenue, so Robert had remained in the family home, with John also commemorated on the Strandtown War Memorial, Belmont Road, Belfast.

Albert Edward Baxter - D-976 - born around 1884, Baxter enlisted into the Royal Engineers (Service Number 57649, 121st Field Company) on 28 November 1914 within four months of war being declared and, after training, was posted to France with the British Expeditionary Force (BEF) on 4 October 1915, where he stayed for just over one year. His next posting was back to the Home Service until he was discharged on 24 December 1917 with an unspecified sickness, being awarded the Silver War Badge. Albert, a tailor by trade, married Margaret McFarlane in St Anne's Church, Belfast on 8 July 1907. Albert died on 16 February 1960 aged 75, with Margaret dying a couple of months later on 5 April 1960 aged 74, both living at 7 Harkness Parade, Belfast at the time of their deaths.

Michael Alfred King - C-2256 - King was recorded as living at 49 Connswater Street, Belfast when he died on 20 February 1965 aged 67, with his headstone stating that he was a 'POW WW1'. This plot also contains Sarah Elizabeth King who was living at 70 Brandon Parade, Belfast when she died on 10 February 1974 aged 70, and Edward Henry King of 57 Orangefield Road, Belfast who died on 19 August 1979 aged 53.

John Smyth - T-873 - '21st Canadian Inf. Battalion Died 8th October 1970 of war wounds' aged 82 whilst living at 6 Batley Street, Belfast. It is interesting to note that Smyth is commemorated as dying 'of war wounds', even though he died aged 82 and 52 years after the end of the Great War. Also buried in this plot is John's 'beloved wife' Margaret Smyth who died on 1 February 1980 aged 88 whilst also living at 6 Batley Street, as well as Joseph McAllister who was living at 13 Glenallen Street, Belfast when he died on 17 February 1995 aged 78, and Margaret McAllister who died at Kingsway Nursing Home, Dunmurry when she died on 19 May 2005 aged 92.

Edgar Lean - T-483 - a plaque on this striking wooden cross reads 'Born-Belfast 20.01.1896 Died-Belfast 17.11.1971. WW1-age 19 Rifleman-Royal Irish Rifles The Somme-Ypres 11.11.1915-03.03.1919. WW2-age 43 Gunner-Royal Artillery North Africa (Tobruk-El Alamein) 21.09.1939-10.9.1945'. The logos of both the Royal Irish Rifles and the Royal Artillery feature on this plaque. For his service in Tobruk (Libya) and El Alamein (Egypt) whilst serving with the Royal Artillery 315 AA Battery (Scottish Horse), Lean was awarded the Africa Star Defence Medal War Medal. Described by his grandson Joe as 'a most remarkable man. Very quiet and reserved', Lean was living at 57 Beresford Street, Belfast when he died aged 75. Also buried in this plot is Edgar's sister Linda Lean 'Born 1900 Died 1988', who was living at 101 Malvern Way, Belfast when she died on 14 November 1988 aged 88.

James (Jimmy) Stewart - R-789 - born on 6 August 1918, the son of John Stewart and Ethel Selina Stewart (née Hayes) of Shankill Road, Belfast, Leading Aircraftman James Stewart served in the Royal Air Force during the Second World War enlisting on 11 January 1939 and serving until 19 February 1946, seeing action in Burma. Leading Aircraftman Stewart served as a Flight Mechanic in RAF 267 Squadron - The 'Pegasus' Squadron. Stewart, 'a dearly beloved husband and father', died on 11 April 1999 aged 80 whilst living at 12 Hamel Court, Castlereagh, with 'his beloved wife Jonathena [Ena] a devoted mother' dying on 21 November 2011.

Trail 9 – Military

This trail is sponsored by my friend Jim Hamilton, one of Sandy Row's finest now living in exile in Comber, and Jim's sponsorship is especially appropriate as he has a keen interest in military matters.

Trail 9 features those who served in the military since the World Wars, and includes those killed in conflicts or accidents whilst serving in the Forces, and features a number of members of the Ulster Defence Regiment (UDR) killed during 'The Troubles'.

Robert McComb - T-1842 - this military headstone, with, unusually, the Ulster Defence Regiment logo coloured in, commemorates 'Private R. McComb Ulster Defence Regiment 23rd July 1972 aged 21', with a plaque at the base of the headstone 'in loving memory of Bobby Murdered 23rd July 1972'. McComb, a member of the UDR, living at 11

Denmark Street, Belfast, was killed whilst off-duty by the IRA and was found shot dead at Kerrera Street, Ardoyne, Belfast. Also interred in this grave and remembered on the plaque is Samuel McComb who died on 26 June 1976 aged 65, and Violet McComb who died on 12 July 1983 aged 68, both also living at 11 Denmark Street at the time of their deaths. Andrew (Drew) McComb is also buried in this grave living at Apt 505-3160 Jaguar Valley, Mississauga, Ontario, Canada when he died on 15 April 1989 aged 33 and was buried on 5 June 1989.

Ranger Ernest M. Costello - T-2138 - 'A dear son and loved brother killed on active service in West Germany 28th March 1973 aged 21 years'. A Royal Irish Rangers logo is at the top of this headstone, with Costello's local address recorded as 58 Howard Street South, Belfast when he was buried on 5 April 1973. Also buried in this plot is Joan Costello who was also living at 58 Howard Street South at the time of her death on 15 August 1984 aged 55, and Charles Henry Costello who was living at 4 Walnut Street, Donegall Pass, Belfast when he died on 30 March 1992 aged 67.

Joseph (Jack) Walden - T-4061 - 'Ex. Arm. Sergt. Northumberland Fus And R.A.C. Born Birmingham Died 2 December 1974 aged 83 years' whilst living at 1 Marlborough Park North, Belfast. In 1968 The (Royal) Northumberland Fusiliers were amalgamated with the Royal Fusiliers (City of London Regiment), the Royal Warwickshire Fusiliers and Lancashire Fusiliers to form the present Royal Regiment of Fusiliers, whilst R.A.C. stands for the Royal Armoured Corps.

Charles Green - T-2428 - this American war grave commemorates 'Charles E. Green ACI US Navy Vietnam 1941 1975'. Charles was registered as living at 8 Glandore Parade, Belfast when he died on 20 August 1975 aged 40, and was buried on 27 August 1975. Whilst not unique in Northern Ireland with a number of such graves in other local cemeteries, I think this is the only American war grave in Roselawn Cemetery.

Gerald William David Tucker - S-681 - this military headstone commemorates Tucker who was shot dead by the IRA shortly after leaving his workplace at the Royal Victoria Hospital, Falls Road, Belfast on 8 June 1977. Tucker, a part-time member of the UDR, was living at 57 Ainsworth Street, Belfast when he died aged 36. Also interred in this grave, and commemorated on a plaque at the base of the headstone, is Charlotte

Emma Tucker who was living at 204 Ballysillan Road, Belfast when she died on 24 August 1994 aged 91.

Private Colin H. Quinn - V-1573 - '3 U.D.R. Killed by terrorist action 10th December 1980 Aged 20 years'. Quinn was a part-time Private with the Ulster Defence Regiment's A. Company, and was shot by the INLA as he left his work in a printing firm in Belfast, with his brother witnessing the killing. Quinn was living at 2 Killynure Close, Carryduff at the time of his death.

Sergeant Dennis Taggart - S-1532 - 'murdered by the I.R.A. 4th August 1986'. Denis (33) was a member of the UDR, and was shot dead outside his home at 42 Battenberg Street, Shankill, Belfast. The base of this headstone states 'He died for what he believed in'. Also buried in this grave is Dennis' 'baby son Simon. Born 16th February 1976 died aged 9 weeks' on 19 April 1976, whilst registered as living at 8f Forthriver Crescent, Belfast.

Stephen Llewellyn - R-769 - Llewellyn was based at Royal Irish Rangers Ballymena, and was shot dead on 22 May 1986 as a result of a Negligent Discharge (ND) of a weapon at Magilligan Camp, county Londonderry. Llewellyn, who was aged 17, came from a family with long military connections.

Steven William Megrath - R-725 - 'murdered by terrorists 17-9-87 aged 20 years'. A member of the Ulster Defence Regiment, whose logo is at the top of this headstone, Private Megrath was killed by the IRA when shot, off duty, while in a relative's home on Halliday's Road, Tiger's Bay, Belfast. Megrath was living at 28 Cameronian Drive, Belfast when he died.

Paul Cree - D-468 - this military headstone commemorates 'Bombardier Paul Frederick Cree 102 AD Regt. R.A. (Y) 5 February 1988 age 23. 30 September 1964 - 5 February 1988. Gone but not forgotten'. Cree was living at 30 Lysander Park, Newtownards at the time of his death. Also buried in this plot, and commemorated on a plaque at the base of the headstone, is William Lee Cree who was living at 21 Parkgate Parade, Belfast when he died on 8 November 1958 aged 51, and Margaret Cree who was living at 18 Slievemore Avenue, Newtownards when she died on 19 December 1978 aged 75.

Allen Lister - D-1468 - 'Traveller, Historian, Philosopher and Soldier died on 4 January 1989' aged 57 whilst living at 25 Belle Bashford Court, Belfast. Also interred in this grave is Samuel Henry Lister who died on 12 October 1957 aged 55, and Martha Lister who died on 1 October 1971 aged 65, both whilst living at 70 Palestine Street, Belfast.

Sergeant Major Frederick Nelson Mullan - R-3316 - 'a devoted husband and dad Frederick Nelson Born 30-7-51 - Died 19-11-91', Mullan was aged 40 when he died whilst registered as living at 33 Geary Road, Belfast and was buried on 29 November 1991, suggesting that he was serving overseas at the time of his death. The top of the headstone features the logo of the Royal Artillery, colloquially known as 'The Gunners', with the base stating 'Lovingly Remembered'. Also buried in this grave is William Mullan who died on 30 June 1999 aged 76, and William Thomas Mullan who died on 24 December 2010 aged 62, both whilst also registered as living at 33 Geary Road.

John Holmberg - R-3638 - 'SGM [Sergeant Major] US Army Korea Vietnam Jun 7 1931 Nov 19 1992 Bronze Star Medal'. The Bronze Star Medal is a United States decoration awarded to members of the United States Armed Forces for either heroic achievement, heroic service, meritorious achievement, or meritorious service in a combat zone. Holmberg was living at 125 Kilcoole Park, Belfast when he died on 19 November 1992 aged 61. Also buried in this grave is 'Alice beloved wife of John 27th March 1924 - 9th Oct. 1998' aged 74 whilst also living at 125 Kilcoole Park.

Stanley Butterwood - P-780 - 'Precious memories of my dearest Stan a loving husband, our devoted dad and grandad Died 10th January 1994 aged 43 years'. Butterwood was living at 18 Woodbreda Park, Castlereagh when he died, with his headstone containing the logos of the Royal Catering Corps '1966-1978' and the Ulster Defence Regiment '1978-1993', with a separate plaque at the grave commemorating 'Stanley Butterwood Masterchef - Soldier'.

Stephen John Thompson - P-1207 - commemorated on this military headstone as a 'Staff Sergeant Royal Electrical and Mechanical Engineers [died] 30 June 1995 aged 31', Thompson was registered as living at 22 Kinross Avenue, Tullycarnet when he died. His headstone also commemorates 'A beloved son brother fiancé uncle and grandson. Remembered forever. Sleep well', with Thompson also commemorated on a plaque at the base of the headstone reading 'Stephen Forever young'.

Lynne Burbidge - P-277 - this military headstone commemorates 'Margaret L. Burbidge ASO40671 Royal Air Force [died] 25th August 1995 - age 42', whilst registered as living at 35 Wallasey Park, Belfast. The base of the headstone states '"Unto thee o Lord, do I lift up my soul" Psalm 25 Verse 1'. A plaque at the base of the headstone also remembers 'Lynne beloved daughter and sister. Precious memories'.

James Roxborough - P-1702 - 'Royal Irish Rifles 6th Airborne Division. 21st Dec 1923 - 5 Sept 1998. This stone was laid in his memory by the Parachute Regimental Association Northern Ireland Branch', with the plaque containing the logos of the Parachute Regiment. Roxborough was aged 74 when he died whilst registered as living 107 Island Street, Belfast.

Reginald (Reg) Hyslop - P-2429 - 'loving husband of Jean, devoted father and grandfather died 21st September 1998 aged 73 years', whilst registered as living at 2 Annadale Green, Belfast. This headstone contains images of the Burma Star, a military campaign medal instituted in May 1945 for award to British and Commonwealth forces who served in the Burma Campaign from 1941 to 1945 during the Second World War. Also remembered on this headstone is 'Eliza Jane (Jean) a devoted wife, mum, gran, and great gran died 7th November 2016 aged 86 years. In our hearts forever', with the base of the headstone stating 'I am the clouds that race above, Where I watch over those I love'.

Connor Lilley - P 2674 - 'Our beloved son and brother Born 1st September 1979 Died 26th October 1998 whilst serving with the Irish Guards in Canada'. This headstone features a photo of Lilley above the words 'GDSM C. Lilley 25058631', with an Irish Guards logo at the top of this headstone. Lilley's home address was recorded as 6 Ravensdale Street, Belfast when he died aged 19 and he was buried on 3 November 1998. A plaque on a seat beside this double headstone commemorates 'Precious memories of a very special person'.

Paul R Cochrane - P-3100 - 18-year-old Royal Irish Regiment trooper Paul Cochrane took his own life at Drumadd Barracks, Armagh on 30 July 2001. Paul's father Billy was speaking to his son on the telephone when he heard a shot being fired. He believes it was the shot that killed Paul. Paul's parents said that in letters their son wrote to them, he said he was being subjected to a campaign of bullying. Along with four families whose sons died at the Deepcut barracks in Surrey, the family joined a campaign to lobby the Ministry of Defence to call for an independent inquiry into apparent suicides of young soldiers.

Lance Corporal John Richard Murphy - W-512 - 'Royal Army Veterinary Corps 7th January 2007 aged 32', with the base of this Commonwealth War Grave-like headstone commemorating 'a loving husband, son and daddy who died as he lived, protecting others. At peace'. Lance Corporal Murphy was living at 71 Moyard Gardens, Greenisland when, suffering from PTSD following service in

Afghanistan, he took his own life leaving a widow Rachel, and two children Emily and Steven.

Scott Robert Hamilton - W-1399 - this military headstone commemorates 'Sapper Scott Hamilton Corps of Royal Engineers 11th February 2010 age 22', with his location of death listed as Masserene Barracks, Randalstown Road, Antrim. The base of the headstone commemorates 'a loving son and brother best friend to many. Gone but never forgotten. RIP'. A bench nearby also commemorates Sapper Hamilton.

Trail 10 – Royal Ulster Constabulary

This trail is sponsored by my good friend Russell Grant, and is especially relevant as this chapter features Mark Bassett with whom Russell grew up.

Sadly there is no shortage of Royal Ulster Constabulary fatalities buried in Roselawn Cemetery to chose from. The majority of officers featured in this chapter were killed as a result of terrorist action, with other officers also featured in the 'Troubles Victims - Bombings' section.

Victor William Arbuckle - U-1 - 'a dear husband and father died 11th October 1969, from gunshot wounds received whilst serving with the R.U.C', aged 29. The first of 302 RUC officers to be killed during 'The Troubles', Arbuckle was one of three people shot dead in the Shankill area of Belfast on 11 October 1969. Victor was shot by the Ulster Volunteer Force (UVF) while two Protestant civilians, George Dickie and Herbert Hawe, were gunned down by the Army. Constable Arbuckle was shot as he stood beside other officers, including Sergeant Dermot Hurley who was shot dead by the IRA just two years later, the first Roman Catholic RUC officer to be killed in 'The Troubles'. Mr Arbuckle's wife Dorothy spoke about her memories of her husband 50 years after his murder; 'We were both very, very happy. He was so proud of his son. I will never forget him. I think about him every day – how things would have been so different if he had been alive today'. Dorothy never remarried, and went on to form a support group for other RUC wives who lost their husbands.

John Haslett - T-34 - 'killed on duty 15th October 1971 aged 21 years'. Haslett was killed by the IRA when shot from a passing car while sitting in a stationary RUC car at the junction of Woodvale Road and Twaddell Avenue, Belfast. Haslett was registered as living at 31 Russell Park, Gilnahirk when he died. Buried in the neighbouring grave - T-35 - is Cecil Cunningham, killed in the same incident. Cecil was living at 51 Westway Gardens, Belfast at the time of his death and was aged 46.

David Montgomery - U-668 - 'died of gunshots wounds received in the execution of his duty at Londonderry 27th Jan. 1972, aged 20 years'. Montgomery was shot dead during an IRA gun attack on his RUC patrol car on the Creggan Road, Derry. Also killed during the same attack was his fellow officer Peter Gilgunn (26). Montgomery was living at 6 Avondale Street, Belfast at the time of his death, having been predeceased by his mother Letitia (Teenie) Montgomery who died on 7 January 1967 aged 43 whilst living at 11 Baywood Street, Belfast. Also buried in this plot is Montgomery's father, David John Montgomery who died on 13 January 2006 aged 83 whilst also living at 6 Avondale Street. The base of this headstone states 'It is not for us to understand but to leave it all in Jesus['s] hands'.

Robert Stuart Nicholl - T-53 - 'Died 13th October 1972 aged 22 years'. An off-duty RUC officer, Nicholl was accidentally shot dead by the Army while driving a car along Castle Street, Belfast. Nicholl was registered as living at 53 Garnerville Park, Belfast at the time of his death. Also buried in this grave is Margaret Martha Nicholl who was also living at 53 Garnerville Park when she died on 15 December 2005 aged 74, and William Nicholl who died on 1 March 2012.

Paul Redcliffe Gray - T-2461 - 'Died on active duty 10th May 1975 aged 20 years'. Gray was shot by an IRA sniper while on RUC foot patrol in Waterloo Street, Derry, with his home address recorded as 4 Brucevale Park, Belfast at the time of his death. The base of the headstone states 'he died as he lived, everyone's friend'. Also buried in this grave is Paul's father Hugh Gray who died on 29 March 1988 aged 58, and his mother Georgina Major Gray who died on 10 January 1994 aged 65, both whilst living at 4 Pomona Avenue, Belfast.

James William Blakely - S-986 - Sergeant Blakely was 'killed in the execution of his duty' on 6 February 1976 when, along with Inspector William Henry Murtagh buried in the neighbouring grave S-987, he was shot dead from behind by terrorist gunmen while on foot patrol on the Cliftonville Road, Belfast. Sergeant Blakely was living at 2 Glenwell Park, Belfast when he died aged 42. Also commemorated on this headstone is 'his darling son Elmer died 4th September 1978 aged 19 yrs', whilst living at 34 Carolsteen Avenue, Helens Bay. Inspector Murtagh is also recorded as 'killed in the execution of his duty' on 6 February 1976, and was living at 48 Cumberland Road, Dundonald when he died aged 31.

Ronald (Ronnie) Edwin McAdam - T-4352 - 'died 2nd June 1976 aged 31 years'. Detective Constable McAdam was shot dead by the IRA whilst off-duty accompanying a patient outside the Royal Victoria Hospital, Falls Road, Belfast. Another member of the Force - Reserve Constable Colin Dunlop - who was also shot dead at the Royal Hospital features later in this chapter. McAdam was registered as living at 5d

Willowbrook House, Belfast at the time of his death. Also buried in this grave is Ronnie's father Joseph who died on 22 June 1986, and his mother Mattie who 'died 13th July 2014'.

Paul Moore Gray - D-1588 - 'killed in action 17th April 1979 aged 25 years'. Gray was killed by a remote controlled bomb hidden in a parked van which was detonated when his RUC mobile patrol drove past in Bessbrook, county Armagh. Gray was recorded as living at 36 Cabinhill Gardens, Belfast at the time of his death. Also killed in the same attack were Gray's RUC colleagues Richard Baird (28), Noel Webb (30) and Robert Lockhart (44). A hall in Knock Presyterian Church in named in Paul's memory. Also buried in this grave is Gray's father James Moore Gray who died on 17 July 1971 aged 54, and John Reid who died on 16 December 1990 aged 82, both whilst also living at 36 Cabinhill Gardens, and Dorothy Gray who died on 26 August 2012.

Derek Kerr Davidson - S-3613 - 'died 2nd August 1979 aged 26 years murdered in the execution of his duty'. Constable Davidson was shot by an IRA sniper when his RUC patrol was lured to the scene of a bogus robbery at Clondara Street, Falls, Belfast. Constable Davidson was living at 121 Kilcoole Park, Belfast at the time of his death. Constable Davidson is the sole occupant of this grave.

Brian Harris - V-1064 - this headstone, which features an RUC logo at the top, was erected 'in loving memory of a beloved son and brother Brian died 28 October 1980'. Reserve Constable Harris was fatally injured when the police Landrover he was travelling in collided with a lorry in Belfast city centre. Also killed in the same incident were his colleagues Joanne Margaret Best, 21, Patrick Francis X. Collins, 34, Paul Mason, 20, and Norman G. Montgomery, 22, with the latter officers buried in Bangor Clandeboye Cemetery and Carrick Victoria Cemetery respectively. Harris was aged 23, and was living at 12 Burntollett Way, Cregagh, at the time of his death. Also commemorated on this headstone is 'his dear sister Alice Jones [who] died 14th August 2015 and his devoted mother Nellie (Nell) [who] died 4th January 2017 aged 101 years'.

Colin P Dunlop - V-1275 - beneath the Royal Ulster Constabulary logo, this headstone, in the shape of an open book, remembers 'Res Const Colin Dunlop died 31st May 1981'. Dunlop (30) was shot by the IRA while guarding a patient at the Royal Victoria Hospital, Falls Road, Belfast, with his home address recorded as 1 Leven Park, Tullycarnet at the time of his death. Also buried in this grave is Patrick Dunlop who died on 30 November 1996 aged 79 whilst living at Arlington Nursing Home, North Parade, Belfast, and Bridget Dunlop who was living at Rowallane Residential Home, Saintfield when she died on 31 December 1999 aged 83. Each occupant of the grave, plus 'June Dunlop died 28th Mar 1994', is remembered in a verse at the base of the headstone stating 'On their souls sweet Jesus have mercy'.

David Brown - C-63 - this headstone commemorates a 'beloved son David Sgt R.U.C. Dear husband of Marjorie Died 16th April 1982 in the service of his country'. Sergeant Brown died two weeks after being shot by the IRA while travelling to the New Barnsley Army / RUC base at Springfield Crescent, off Springfield Road, Belfast. Sergeant Brown was living at 31 Loopland Park, Belfast when he died aged 35, and was predeceased by his mother Flora Ann Brown who was living at 29 Severn Street, Belfast when she died on 27 October 1963 aged 57.

Edward Gordon Dunning - S-3004 - 'born 11th August 1946 Died 16 January 1983' aged 36. Constable Dunning of 9 Lowland Walk, Tullycarnet died of natural causes whilst serving with the Royal Ulster Constabulary, with the force's logo at the top of his headstone. Also buried in this plot are 'devoted parents and grandparents Molly, Born 25th January 1922 Died 1st May 1993 aged 71', and 'Jack, Born 26th May 1919 Died 25th March 2001 aged 81', both whilst also living at 9 Lowland Walk.

Edward Magill - V-2203 - 'Res. Constable R.U.C. called home 20 Feb. 1983 aged 20 years', whilst recorded as living at 68 Glencairn Crescent, Belfast. Reserve Constable Magill was shot from a passing car by the IRA while he was standing outside the RUC base in Warrenpoint, county Down. Also buried in this grave is Barbara Magill 'a dearly beloved wife and precious mother called home 6th Jan. 1995' aged 62 whilst recorded as living at 25 Abbeydale Park, Belfast. The base of this headstone states 'The Lord gave and the Lord hath taken'.

Michael William Todd - U-1794 - 'Murdered in the execution of his duties 15th June 1984 aged 22 years'. Constable Todd was shot by an Irish National Liberation Army (INLA) gunman during a gun battle after RUC members surrounded a house in Lenadoon Avenue, Belfast. Constable Todd was shot as he searched a flat, and was living at 17 Hillview Gardens, Moss Road, Lambeg at the time of his death. He was posthumously awarded the Queen's Gallantry Medal. His mother, Elizabeth Todd who 'died 7th February 2013' and is buried in the same plot, said the Queen's subsequent presentation of the George Cross to the RUC had been very important to her; 'It was a great honour to me and my daughter. We both felt he deserved it for his bravery and what he had done for the community. I find it hard to describe, but he enjoyed his work so much and for his bravery I believe he deserved it'. Also buried in this plot is Sarah Barnes who was living at 5 Syringa Street, Belfast when she died on 22 January 1967 aged 74, and William James Todd who was also living at 17 Hillview Gardens when he died on 10 October 1973 aged 43.

Derek Ewing Patterson - R-679 - 'Dearly loved husband of Anne and father of Derek, Victoria and Ryan Murdered 10th November 1986'. An RUC crest at the top of this red headstone with gold lettering remembers Patterson who was shot by the Irish People's Liberation Organisation (IPLO), off duty, outside a friend's home on Fitzroy Avenue, off Ormeau Road, Belfast. Patterson was living at 55 Wandsworth Road, Belfast when he died aged 39.

Paul McCullough - R-2399 - 'Const Paul McCullough QGM [Queen's Gallantry Medal] aged 29 years. Beloved husband of Sharon and devoted father of Clare and Steven Died 25 October 1988'. Constable McCullough, of 20 Oakdale, Ballygowan, was fatally injured in a motorcycle accident when travelling to work. A Royal Ulster Constabulary logo is at the top of this headstone, with the words 'Lovingly Remembered' at the base of the headstone.

Campbell - R-3446 - this headstone, with an RUC logo at the top, was erected 'in loving memory of Constable John Thomas Aged 31 years Also his dear Wife W/Constable [Women Constable] Karin Jacqueline aged 26 years Killed on the 8th January 1989 In British Midlands Air Disaster Kegworth'. The Campbells were living at 15 Ardmore Heights, Ballygowan when they died. As mentioned in Trail 13 detailing the Moloneys buried in the neighbouring grave R-3446, the disaster occurred when a British Midland Boeing 737-400 crashed onto a motorway embankment while attempting to make an emergency landing at East Midlands Airport.

Mark Kenneth Bassett - R-3053 - Constable Bassett died on 20 June 1990, aged 20, after he was fatally injured in a road traffic accident when travelling to duty in Omagh, county Tyrone. Bassett was a friend of chapter sponsor Russell Grant, with his headstone containing the logos of both the Salvation Army and the Royal Ulster Constabulary, with the base of the headstone stating 'He went in the strength of the Lord'. Bassett played rugby for the Civil Service and previously for the Ulster under 18s, and was a member of the Belfast Temple Salvation band where he played the cornet. Constable Bassett also won an award during his police training before his untimely death.

Samuel Todd - R-2970 - 'Died 15th October 1990 Aged 40 Years Beloved husband of Maureen. Adoring Dad of Geoffrey and Christopher. Unselfish in life. Unselfish in death'. Todd, of 54 Ballydrain Road, Comber, died two days after being shot by the IRA while sitting in an RUC civilian type van at a security barrier in High Street, Belfast. The RUC logo is on the top of this headstone, with a dog either side, suggesting that Todd was a police dog handler, with the bottom of the headstone reading, 'Only you know how much I love you'. Tragically Todd's wife Maureen '4th July 1951 to 9th August 2000. Dearly beloved wife and mother, caring and thoughtful friend. Deeply regretted and sadly missed' is also buried in this plot, living at 17 Waddles Hill, Comber at the time of her death, with the base of the headstone stating 'Safe and at peace - no more pain'.

Joan Elizabeth McFall - W-666 - below a Royal Ulster Constabulary logo, this headstone states 'Born 21.1.1958, Died 11.4.2007 Joanie to Colin, Mum to Julie and Craig', with McFall living at 1 Mill Road, Ballygowan at the time of her death aged 48, with the base of this headstone stating "Courage is, with love, the greatest gift".

Trail 11 – Troubles Victims: Shot

This trail is sponsored by the award-winning DC Tours, the creation of Mark Wylie and Paul Donnelly, and whose tours I would thoroughly recommend. Book online at www.deadcentretours.com.

Sadly there are so many victims of 'The Troubles' buried in Roselawn that I have had to devise two trails dedicated to a selection of the victims - Trail 11 features those who were shot dead, with 1972 being an especially brutal year.

Thomas John (Jackie) Todd - U-2513 - 'who lost his life through gun shot wounds on 8th Sept. 1969 while attempting to maintain peace during the riots in Belfast'. Todd (27) was one of the earliest victims of 'The Troubles' and was shot during street disturbances in Alloa Street in the Lower Oldpark area of Belfast. Todd was living at 8 Suir Street, Belfast at the time of his death. Also buried in this plot is Margaret Baxter who was living at 23 Suir Street when she died on 10 July 1962 aged 65.

Robert Neill - D-370 - Neill (38) of 18 Central Street, Belfast was shot dead by the IRA during street disturbances at the junction of Central Street and Newtownards Road, Belfast on 27 June 1970 during what became known as 'The Battle of St Matthews'. James McCurrie (34) was also killed at Beechfield Street, Short Strand, Belfast during the incident, and both men are commemorated at a memorial garden on the Newtownards Road, Belfast not far from the location of their deaths.

Orr - T-258 - 'Our beloved sons Malcolm (Junior) 20 years Peter (Pete) 19 years Found shot 5th July 1972'. The Orr brothers were found shot dead by the side of the road at Carnaghliss, near Dundrod, both living at 66 Alliance Road, Belfast at the time of their deaths. The brothers' supposed 'crime' was that they were socialising with girls from a Roman Catholic background. Barbaric. This heart-shaped headstone also commemorates 'their dear father Francis 49 years Died 14th April 1977', with the base of this headstone stating 'Always remembered'.

David Andrews - T-275 - 'our dear son David killed by a terrorist bullet 9th July 1972' aged 31. Andrews was found shot dead at the Waterworks, off the Cavehill Road, Belfast. At the time of his death, Andrews was living at 14 Heathfield Drive, Belfast. Tragically ten other civilians also lost their lives on 9 July 1972 including Joseph Flemming (30), Brian McMillan (21), Alan Meehan (18), Angelo Fionda (60), and Gerald Turkington (32) all killed in separate incidents, whilst Catholic Priest Noel Fitzpatrick (40), John Dougal (16), Margaret Gargan (13), Patrick Butler (38) and David McCafferty (15) were all shot by an Army sniper from an observation post in Corry's Timber Yard, while in the vicinity of Westrock Drive, Ballymurphy, Belfast. Horrendous.

William J. McIlwrath Moore - C-2248 - 'died 6th September 1972 aged 20 years. Result of gunshot wounds'. Moore was shot from a passing car while walking along Castlereagh Street, Belfast, whilst registered as living at 44 Highcairn Drive, Belfast. Also buried in this grave is Moore's mother Emma Beatrice Moore who died on 28 December 1992 aged 69, and his father Isaac Moore who died on 24 June 1996 aged 73, both whilst living at 25 Castleward Park, Belfast.

Trevor William Rankin - T-3260 - 'died 5th Jan. 1973 Aged 18 years Innocent victim of terrorist shooting'. Rankin was shot dead by the IRA at Ben Madigan filling station, Shore Road, Belfast when he was mistaken for an off duty Ulster Defence Regiment member. Also interred in this plot is Trevor's father William Rankin who died on 24 July 1990 aged 65, and his mother Sarah Rankin who died on 12 June 1995 aged 70, all three living at 7 Dublin Street, Belfast at the time of their deaths.

George Walmsley - T-2157 - 'Bro George Walmsley, Secretary Murdered 2nd March 1973 when leaving Ligoniel Orange Hall by the I.R.A'. This headstone, 'erected by L.O.L. 1891', commemorates George

(52) who had served in the Merchant Navy and then worked as a foreman for the Belfast Corporation, who was shot shortly after leaving the Orange Hall on the Ligoniel Road, Belfast leaving the meeting early to be with his mother following his father's death less than a fortnight earlier. Also buried in this grave is George's father William Wamsley who died on 21 February 1973 aged 86, and his mother Emily who died on 31 January 1976 also aged 86, with all three recorded as living at 69 Glenbank Drive, Belfast at the time of their deaths.

Norman Hutchinson - T-3428 - 'died 12th August 1973 result of gun shot wounds aged 17 years'. Hutchinson, who was living at 45 Kilbroney Bend, Cregagh, Belfast was shot by the UVF while walking along Ormeau Road, near University Street, Belfast. Also buried in this plot is 'his devoted mother' Doris Hutchinson who died on 31 March 1982 aged 51 whilst also living at Kilbroney Bend, and John 'a devoted husband, father and grandfather died 30th December 2015'. The base of the headstone states 'The Lord is my shepherd bear ye one anothers burdens'.

Hugh McVeigh - T-4184 - 'a devoted husband and father murdered April 1975'. McVeigh, a member of the UDA, was killed by the UVF. Abducted while delivering furniture somewhere in the Shankill area of Belfast on information supplied to the British authorities, McVeigh was found shot and buried on wasteland at The Gobbins, Islandmagee on 1 September 1975. Fellow UDA member David Douglas was also killed in the same incident and is buried at Plot U-1117 where he is commemorated as 'a beloved son .. murdered April 1975'. Both men were buried on 5 September 1975. McVeigh was living at 8 Cumnock Walk, Ballybeen, Dundonald when he died aged 38, whilst 20-year-old Douglas was living at 42 Grove Street East, Belfast. Also buried in U-1117 is Elizabeth Douglas who was also living at 42 Grove Street East when she died on 17 September 1970 aged 45, and Robert Henry Douglas who was living at 34 Jonesboro Park, Belfast when he died on 14 April 2002 aged 83.

Robert McCartney Shields - S-3243 - 'Robin (Ambulance Officer) Murdered by the I.R.A. 30th September 1980'. The top of this headstone contains a NI Ambulance Service logo, with Shields living at 27 Woodvale Road, Belfast at the time of his death aged 44. According to the journalist Ivan Little in an article in the Belfast Telegraph in 2008, 'for some inexplicable reason, one funeral out of all the hundreds I have attended still plays in my mind as if it were yesterday. Robin Shields, who had been in the police reserve, was shot dead by the IRA in September 1980. He died at his desk in the ambulance depot of the Royal Victoria Hospital. The grief as his coffin was brought from his home in the Woodvale area of Belfast was so overpowering, so intense, that I had to walk away. To cap it all, a series of IRA bomb scares held up the funeral, causing some mourners to miss the burial at Roselawn cemetery'.

John D Smith - V-1509 - 'Private J.D. Smith The Ulster Defence 'R'[Regiment died] 27th March 1981 aged 26'. Private Smith was shot dead by the IRA while on his way to work at Cromac Street in the Markets area of Belfast. Smith was living at 30 North Bank, Cregagh, Belfast at the time of his death. Also interred in this plot is John's mother Alice Smith who was also living at 30 North Bank when she died on 7 July 2001 aged 63.

Kenneth Campbell - V-1951 - Campbell was the caretaker at a community centre in Finaghy and was shot dead when the IRA also killed Reverend Roy Bradford whilst he was hosting a political surgery at the centre on 14 November 1981. Campbell was living at 15 Geeragh Place, Finaghy at the time of his death aged 29. Also buried in this plot is Kenneth's mother Florence Annie Campbell who was also living at 15 Geeragh Place when she died on 8 July 1991 aged 71. Rev. Bradford was an ordained Methodist Minister and an Ulster Unionist Member of Parliament for the Belfast South constituency. After Rev. Bradford's funeral service at Dundonald Presbyterian Church - conducted by Rev. Roy Magee, as featured in Trail 18 - NI Secretary of State, Jim Prior was verbally abused and jostled by a group of angry loyalists, before Rev. Bradford's interment in Ballyvester Cemetery, Donaghadee.

Children sob for 'Uncle Ken'

SOBBING schoolchildren shared in grief yesterday at the funeral of community worker Ken Campbell.

Young girls held tearful friends in their arms as the cortege left a funeral parlour on the Lisburn Road. Mr Campbell (29), who ran Finaghy Community Centre, was buried as gunmen fled after killing Mr Campbell Saturday.

A group of children from several schools — many who all knew him as a friend 'uncle' and who stayed discos at the centre.

He had been organising a disco when he died and many of the children who were there in terror and hid under the tables when the gunmen burst in were at the funeral. One 15-year-old boy said: "All the children loved Ken. He lived for children. He ran running discos, he took them away on fishing trips. Everybody is terribly

Mr Campbell was unmarried. His three brothers Graham, Billy and Roy, and sister attended the mourners. His widowed mother, was too upset to attend. Party representatives included Official Unionist leader James Molyneaux, DUP deputy leader Ian Paisley, Peter Robinson and Mr McQuade, Alliance Party secretary

tary John Cushnahan, Lord Mayor Councillor Mrs Grace Bannister and her deputy, Councillor Frank Millar.

UDA leader Andy Tyrie was also there. During a brief service at the parlour, Finaghy Baptist Church Pastor George Crory said that Ulster faced its "darkest hour".

He said: "This is a sad day, not only for the family of Mr Campbell, but for the people of Ulster. Kenneth happened to be going about his lawful business and was in the wrong place at the wrong time. We have no need to be filled with despair, in spite of the evil of this attack in this darkest hour the Province faces. If we turn to evil things and evil methods ourselves, then we are defeated. All who carry the gun are dead as they walk the streets. God's judgment is already on them".

He urged people not to take the law into their own hands and said Satan was working through the IRA. Shops were closed and traffic at a standstill during the service and as the cortege moved off towards Roselawn Cemetery. At the graveside, Pastor Crory said: "Allow God to bring justice and retribution to the evil men. Ultimately he will do so. He will not allow them to escape to carry on with impunity. God will judge the IRA."

☐ The funeral cortege of Mr Campbell passing along the Lisburn Road.

Mitchell - S-3831 - this headstone was erected 'in loving memory of Robert (Bobby) a dearly loved husband and father murdered by cowards 23rd January 1982. Also his dearly loved son Roy a much loved brother murdered by cowards 23rd January 1982'. Aged 46 and 21 respectively, the Mitchells were shot at their home, 48 Rosebery Gardens, off Woodstock Road, Belfast during an internal Ulster Defence Association dispute. Also buried in this grave, which has a small UDA symbol at the top of the headstone, is a 'loving wife and mother Martha [and] a devoted Granny died 27th December 2005' whilst living at 30 Cypress Park, Donaghadee, aged 73.

George Seawright - 'Murdered by the enemies of Ulster .... A devoted husband and father. Died 3rd December 1987' aged 36. Born in Glasgow, Seawright lived in Drumchapel and worked in the shipyards of Clydeside. He then worked in the Harland and Wolff shipyard in Belfast until entering politics as a member of the Democratic Unionist Party. As well as being a shipyard worker, Seawright also served as a lay preacher and was an elder in north Belfast's John Knox Memorial Free Presbyterian Church. Seawright was also a member of Ulster Volunteer Force, an Orange Lodge in the Ballysillan area of North Belfast and the Apprentice Boys of Derry. He lived in the unionist Glencairn estate in the northwest of the city, where he was shot dead by the Irish People's Liberation Organisation (IPLO).

James Craig - R-2288 - 'Dear husband of Mary. Devoted father and grandfather. Murdered by a coward 15th October 1988. Here lies a man in a million'. A member of the UDA, Craig was shot by the Ulster Freedom Fighters (UFF) while in The Castle Inn, Beersbridge Road, Belfast during an internal UDA dispute. Craig lived at 14 Northland Street, Belfast at the time of his death aged 46. Also killed in the same incident was Victor Rainey - buried at D-80, where he is recorded as a 'dearly loved son' - who was not the intended target. Rainey was living at 19 Tamery Pass, Belfast at the time of his death aged 68. On 6 January 2001, The Castle Inn (then known as the Bunch of Grapes) was also apparently the location of the torture and murder of George (Geordie) Legge who was found beaten and stabbed to death off the Clontonacally Road, near Carryduff, during an internal UDA dispute. 37-year-old Legge was living at 85 Island Street, Belfast at the time of his death, and is buried at plot P-3198.

Francis Charles Galbraith - R-2724 - 'a loving husband and devoted father Francis murdered 19 April 1989 shot by cowards aged 29 years' whilst registered as living at 49 Inverary Drive, Belfast. Galbraith, a civilian, was shot dead by a non-specific Loyalist group while walking along Park Avenue, off Holywood Road, Belfast. Also buried in this grave 'at peace with her eldest son Frankie [is] Joan beloved wife, mother and grandmother died 25th September 2002 aged 62 years' whilst living at 225 Park Avenue, Belfast. With Park Avenue recorded as the location of Frankie's death, and also his mother's home address, I would suggest that he was on his way to visiting his mother when he was shot dead.

William Kingsberry - R-3614 - 'murdered by I.R.A terrorists 13th November 1991' aged 35, William was a member of the UDA, and was shot dead, together with his stepson, at his home at Lecale Street in the Village area of Belfast. William's stepson, Samuel Mehaffey, is buried in the neighbouring grave - R-3615 - where he is recorded as 'Murdered 13th November 1991 aged 19 years', and was registered as living at 226 Tate's Avenue, Belfast when he died.

Lynn - R-3168 - this headstone commemorates 'John Stephen Lynn Stevie Born 25-12-1960 innocently murdered 13-11-1991' and 'Kenneth William Lynn Kenny Born 13-7-1963 innocently murdered 13-11-1991'. Brothers Kenneth and Stephen Lynn were shot dead by the IRA as they worked on a house on the upper Crumlin Road, Belfast. The two were renovating a bungalow that had previously belonged to a senior UVF man. A third brother in the house at the time survived the shooting. Stevie, 'beloved husband of Michelle Devoted father of Stephen and Kurtis' was living at 8 Wigton Street, Belfast when he died aged 30, whilst Kenny, 'Loved and missed by Gail and daughter Victoria' was living at 8 Ballyutoag Road, Belfast and was aged 28 when he died, with both brothers buried on 6 December 1991.

William McManus - R-1740 - 'in loving memory of my dear husband and our devoted father and grandfather William (Big Willy) murdered 5 February 1992 aged 54'. William was killed by the UFF during a gun attack on Sean Graham's Bookmaker's shop on the Ormeau Road, Belfast. William lived at 62 Shaftesbury Avenue, Belfast at the time of his death. Also killed during the attack was Christy Doherty (52) of 6 Powerscourt Place, Belfast, buried in the neighbouring plot at R-1739, with his headstone stating 'God grant us serenity courage and wisdom', and Jack Duffin (66), James Kennedy (15), and Peter Magee (18). All five victims are remembered on a plaque and memorial at the bookmakers.

Edward (Ned) McCreery - R-4022 - 'a beloved husband, father and grandfather murdered by cowards 14th April 1992 aged 46 years'. McCreery, a member of the UDA, was shot dead by the UFF outside his home at 47 Grahamsbridge Road, Dundonald. It was alleged that

McCreery was an informer. This headstone, which contains a photo of McCreery, states at the bottom 'Gone but not forgotten', with a Canadian flag placed at the base of the headstone, alongside a plaque stating 'Granda McCreery love you always Craig Jonathan and Chloe'.

Margaret Elizabeth Wright - P-976 - 'Born 12th July 1962 Murdered 6th April 1994'. Margaret (31) of 95 Forthriver Park, Belfast, was savagely beaten and shot four times in the head in the Meridi Street band hall in the Donegall Road area of Belfast after being mistaken for a Catholic, with her body discovered by police in a wheelie bin the following day. Wright's headstone represents an open book with the second section stating 'Lord make me a channel of Thy peace', whilst a plaque at this grave reads 'A token of love Jesus paid it all XXX'. While five people were convicted in connection with Wright's horrific death, two men were shot dead when loyalist paramilitaries took action against her killers. Ian Hamilton was killed less than a week later, whilst Billy Elliot, who ran the band hall known as the 'Bad Bet', who ordered the killing, was shot dead by his own organisation, the Red Hand Commando (RHC) on 28 September 1995 aged 31 after returning from Scotland after the loyalist ceasefire in the mistaken belief that he was no longer under threat.

Trail 12 – Troubles Victims: Bombings

This Trail is sponsored by Stewart McCracken who well remembers the terrible events of Bloody Friday.

Trail 12 features those Troubles victims who died as a result of bomb attacks, and includes victims from the explosions at La Mon, Narrow Water and Bloody Friday as mentioned below.

Ernest Bates - T-564 - 'died 29th Sept 1971 Result of an explosion in Four Step Inn'. Ernest (39) was killed along with Alexander Andrews (60) in an explosion at the Four Step Inn on the Shankill Road in Belfast. No group claimed responsibility but it was believed that the attack was perpetrated by the IRA. Ernest was living nearby at 71 Battenberg Street, Belfast at the time of his death, whilst Alexander - buried at T-534, where he is also remembered on the headstone as dying as 'Result of an explosion in Four Step Inn' - was living at 27 Derry Street, Belfast when he died.

Janet Bereen - T-395 - Janet (21) was killed, along with her friend Anne Owens (22), as a result of the Abercorn Restaurant bombing on 4 March 1972. The bomb explosion, which was blamed on the Provisional IRA, also injured more than 130 people. Anne was employed at the Electricity Board, whilst Janet was a hospital radiographer. Also buried in this grave are Janet's parents, Dr James Frederick Bereen who died on 7 October 1987 aged 74, and Eda Bereen who died on 2 June 2002 aged 88, both whilst registered as living at 26 Thornhill, Malone Road, Belfast. It is claimed that Dr Bereen was helping treat casualties from the explosion, and was only told of his daughter's death after he had finished his duties.

Ernest Dougan - T-404 - 'killed 20th March 1972 in Donegall St explosion aged 39 years. Beloved husband of Jean and a dear father'. One of the first car bombs that the IRA used in their armed campaign, seven people were killed in the explosion, including two members of the RUC who were evacuating people to a safe area following misleading telephone calls. Dougan (39) was killed along with fellow Belfast Corporation binmen James Macklin (30) and Samuel Trainor (39). Dougan was living at 231 Tennent Street,

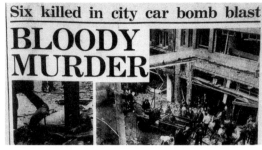

Belfast when he died, whilst Trainor - an off-duty Ulster Defence Regiment soldier and a member of the Orange Order - is buried nearby at T-381, and was living at 58 Northwood Drive, Belfast at the time of his death. The bomb, planted by the Provisional IRA Belfast Brigade, also injured 148 people.

William Kenneth Crothers - F-203 - 'William (Billy) Died 21st July 1972 result of an explosion'. 15-year-old William was killed on Bloody Friday when the IRA detonated at least twenty bombs in the space of eighty minutes, most within a half hour period, in Belfast. The majority of the bombs were car bombs and most targeted infrastructure, especially the transport network. Nine people were killed, while 130 were injured. Crothers was living at 62 Parker Street, Belfast when he died. Also buried in this grave is his father Gilbert Crothers who was also living in 62 Parker Street when he died on 21 September 1965 aged 42, and his mother Everal who died on 30 May 2015. Also killed on Bloody Friday was William (Billy) Irvine, who is buried at T-246 where a heart-shaped headstone was erected 'in memory of our beloved son Billy died 21st July 1972', with a flower holder at the base of the grave commemorating 'Billy killed 21 July 1972'. Billy (18) was registered as living at 5c Glenallen Street, Belfast. Also buried in this grave is Elizabeth Irvine who was living at 13 Epworth Street, Belfast when she died on 6 March 1992

aged 74, and John Irvine who died on 22 January 1997 aged 74 whilst also living at 13 Epworth Street, and Samuel L. Irvine who was living at 17 Trillick Street, Belfast when he died on 4 January 2009 aged 59.

Hugh Harvey - T-2692 - 'our dear son and a beloved brother Hugh killed in an explosion 28th Feb. 1974 aged 34 years'. Harvey, a Protestant, was killed in a UVF bomb attack on the Red Star Bar, Donegall Quay, Belfast, whilst registered as living at 47 Third Street, Belfast. Also buried in this grave is Ethel M. Riddall who died on 25 September 1976 aged 83, John Harvey who died on 13 April 1983 aged 69, and Elizabeth Harvey who died on 14 May 2001 aged 85, all three whilst registered as living at 27 Forthriver Drive, Belfast.

William Andrews - S-1115 - 'died as result of an explosion in the Mountainview Tavern 5th April 1975'. William (Billy) was one of five men killed in the bomb attack on the Mountainview Tavern, Shankill Road, Belfast by the Republican Action Force, believed to be a covername used by the Provisional IRA. Billy, a member of the UDA, was aged 33 at the time of his death whilst living at 49 Glencairn Way, Belfast. The other victims of the attack were Albert Hagan Fletcher, buried nearby at S-1087, who was 32 and living at 85 Disraeli Street, Belfast, Alan Madden (18), Nathaniel Adams (29) and Joseph Bell (52). Earlier in the day, two Catholic civilians, Kevin Kane (18) and Michael Coyle (20) were killed in a bomb attack on McLaughlin's Bar, Antrim Road, New Lodge, Belfast, carried out by the Protestant Action Force, a name used by the Ulster Volunteer Force. Thomas Robinson (61) was shot later the same night by loyalists while walking home from a social club at Etna Drive, Ardoyne, Belfast bringing the death toll to eight on just one day.

Andrew (Andy) Johnston - T-4168 - 'Det Constable. R.U.C. killed in the execution of his duty 7th July 1975 aged 26 years'. A member of the Royal Ulster Constabulary, Johnston was killed by the IRA when a booby trap bomb attached to a desk at Carrick Primary School, Sloan Street, Lurgan, exploded. Johnston was living at 3 Meadowvale,

Waringstown at the time of his death, with the base of his headstone stating 'time passes, memories stay, quietly remembered every day'.

Hughie Harris - T-2429 - 'A dear husband and dad. Murdered by a sectarian assassin 13th August 1975 aged 21 years'. Harris, a member of the UVF living at 105 Palmer Street, Belfast, was killed during an IRA gun and bomb attack on the Bayardo Bar, Shankill Road, Belfast. Civilian victims of the attack on the Bayardo Bar buried in this Cemetery are William John Gracey (63) of 52 Aberdeen Street, Belfast interred at T-4199, Samuel Andrew Gunning (55) of 55 Aberdeen Street, Belfast interred at T-4198, both recorded as 'Died 13th August 1975', and Johanne McDowell (29) of 3 Highburn Crescent, Belfast interred at T-249 (unmarked). Also killed during the attack was Linda Boyle (29), with each of the victims commemorated at a memorial at the scene of the attack, and on a mural nearby.

Daniel Magill - S-481 - 'in loving memory of a dear husband and father Daniel died 17th Feb 1978, aged 37 years. Also his dear wife Mervarid died 18th November 2015'. Magill was killed as a result of The La Mon restaurant bombing, an incendiary bomb attack by the IRA which is described as one of the worst atrocities of the Troubles. The IRA left a large incendiary bomb, containing a napalm-like substance, outside one of the restaurant's windows. There were 450 diners, hotel staff and guests inside the building. The blast created a fireball, killing twelve people and injuring thirty more, many of whom were severely burnt. Magill was living at 68 Cumberland Road, Dundonald at the time of his death aged 37.

Thomas Vance - T-1825 - Vance was a serving member of the Parachute Regiment of the British Army when he was killed in two remote-controlled IRA bomb attacks at Narrow Water, near Warrenpoint, which killed a total of eighteen soldiers on 27 August 1979. The first bomb was left in a parked lorry and detonated when the Army lorry passed, whilst the second bomb was left in a nearby gate lodge and detonated when Army reinforcements arrived at the scene. Vance was living at 21 Molton Drive, Lincoln and was aged 23 at the time of his death. The attacks happened on the same day that the IRA assassinated Lord Mountbatten and three other innocent civilians, in Mullaghmore, county Sligo.

Joseph Rose - T-67 - 'Const. Joseph Rose, 21 years, murdered in the execution of his duty 11 Feb. 1980'. Rose was killed by the IRA in a landmine attack on his RUC mobile patrol on the Lisnaskea Road, near Rosslea, county Fermanagh. Rose was registered as living at 12 Claggan Gardens, Ballybeen at the time of his death. Also buried in this plot is Doreen Rose who was living at 82 Well Road, Ballywalter when she died on 3 May 2009 aged 76.

Constable William Coulter - V-1905 - 'Aged 23 years murdered in the execution of his duty 28th November 1981'. Constable Coulter, of 36 Glencairn Crescent, Belfast, was killed by a remote controlled bomb hidden behind fencing while on RUC foot patrol at Unity Flats, Peter's Hill, Belfast. Also buried in this grave is Robert Coulter who died on 11 December 1997 aged 74, and Eva Anna Coulter who died on 24 June 1998 aged 64, both whilst registered as living at 33 Woodvale Pass, Belfast.

Paul Hamilton - V-2091 - 'aged 25 years murdered in the execution of his duties 27th October 1982. Dear husband of Wendy and father of Simon Paul'. Constable Hamilton was killed, along with his colleagues Sean Quinn (37) and Alan McCloy (34), in an IRA landmine attack on their armoured RUC patrol car at Oxford Island, near Lurgan, county Armagh. Constable Hamilton was living at 29 Dorchester Park, Belfast at the time of his death, with the base of the headstone stating 'Forever in God's keeping. Always in our thoughts'.

Desmond Dobbin - R-542 - 'a dearly loved husband and devoted father killed in the execution of his duty 12th October 1986'. Dobbin (42) was killed in a mortar bomb attack on New Barnsley Army / RUC base on Springfield Road, Belfast, whilst registered as living at 24 Lenaghan Park, Belfast. The top of the headstone contains the Royal Ulster Constabulary logo, with the base stating 'Loved and longed for everyday'.

Peter Nesbitt - R-1188 - Reserve Constable Nesbitt was killed by the IRA when a remote controlled bomb hidden in a derelict shop was detonated as his RUC mobile patrol was lured to a bogus robbery at an adjoining shop at the Ardoyne shops, Crumlin Road, Belfast. Nesbitt, also a draughtsman at Shorts aircraft factory, was living at 13 Woodvale Drive, Belfast when he 'died 10th March 1987' aged 32. Five fellow RUC officers were also injured when a 100lb bomb exploded at Roselawn's main entrance on the same day as Reserve Constable Nesbitt's funeral. Nesbitt's headstone contains the Royal Ulster Constabulary and Scout Association logos as he was also a Scout leader organising an annual camp for disabled children. Also buried in this plot are Peter's parents Margaret Nesbitt who died on 30 January 2000 aged 80, and Nathaniel Nesbitt who died on 19 September 2004 aged 87, both living at 8 Rathgill Court, Bangor at the time of their deaths.

James (Boon) Cummings - S-1016 - 'died 24th February 1988 murdered by the enemies of Ulster'. 22-year-old Private Cummings died shortly after being injured when a remote controlled bomb hidden behind hoardings was detonated when his UDR mobile patrol arrived at a permanent Vehicle Check Point in Royal Avenue, Belfast. Cummings was registered as living at 12 Avonlea Gardens, Rathcoole when he died. Private Fred Starrett also died in this incident and is interred in Dundonald Cemetery at plot D5-494. Boon was predeceased by his grandfather James (senior) who was also living at 12 Avonlea Gardens at the time of his death on 14 December 1975 aged

66. Also buried in this plot is Boon's grandmother Elizabeth 'Lily (Nanny)' who was living at 36 Damascus Street, Belfast when she died on 6 December 1995 aged 83, and his father James who died on 6 June 2005 when registered as living at 104 Omeath Street, Belfast.

Norman McKeown - R-2355 - 'a dear husband and father', McKeown was killed by the IRA on 17 October 1988 aged 39 when a booby trap bomb attached to his car exploded outside his home at 57 Dunleady Park, Dundonald. McKeown's employer was a contractor to the Royal Ulster Constabulary. I lived in Dunleady Park until 1980, and can remember this incident and the shock that that type of atrocity could happen in Dundonald. Also buried in this grave is Evelyn McKeown 'a devoted wife and loving mother' who died on 3 April 2015.

John Bradley - V-2629 - 'L/Cpl John (Brad) Bradley murdered by the I.R.A. with three colleagues 9th April 1990 aged 25 years. Beloved husband of Lauran, father of Aaron and Robyn'. Lance Corporal Bradley was killed, along with fellow UDR members Private John Birch (28), Lance Corporal Michael Adams (23) and Private Steven Smart (23), in a Provisional IRA landmine attack on their mobile patrol on the Ballydugan Road, Downpatrick. They were travelling as part of a two Land Rover patrol from Ballykinlar to Downpatrick when the IRA used a command wire to detonate a 1000lb landmine bomb hidden in a culvert beneath the road which exploded under the men's Land Rover killing them instantly. Four other UDR soldiers in the lead Land Rover were treated for injuries along with two civilians passing by. The force of the explosion was so powerful that it launched the second Land Rover over a hedge and 30 yards into a field and left a crater 50 feet long, 40 feet wide and 15 feet deep. Barbaric. Lance Corporal Bradley was living at 29 Hatton Drive, Belfast at the time of his death.

James and Ellen Sefton - R-3518 - recorded at the base of their headstone as 'Killed by terrorists', the Seftons died when an IRA booby trap bomb attached to their car exploded on 7 June 1990 shortly after they left their home at Lyndhurst Gardens, Belfast, while driving along Ballygomartin Road. James was a retired RUC reservist, with the couple both aged 65 at the time of their deaths. Their son Peter, a high-profile barrister, who defended double-killer Hazel Stewart in court, also called for the murder of his parents to be reinvestigated, alleging that former Sinn Féin deputy first minister Martin McGuinness played a role in ordering the murder.

Robert Skey - R-3126 - 'Died 24th November 1991 aged 27 years Murdered by the enemies of Ulster'. Skey, a member of the UDA with a home address of 22 Denmark Street, Belfast, was killed, along with Colin Caldwell (aged 23, and buried in Carnmoney Cemetery), when a time bomb exploded in the dining hall of 'C' wing in Crumlin Road Prison, Belfast. A UDA logo is at the top of this headstone, with the plot also containing the remains of Emma Agnew Esdale who was living at 37 Tildarg Avenue, Belfast when she died on 22 August 2010 aged 81.

Baird / Morrison - P-60 - 'Murdered in the Shankill Road Bombing 23 October 1993'. Evelyn Baird and Michael Morrison, both aged 27, and their 7-year-old daughter Michelle died during one of the most notorious incidents of the Troubles when the IRA aimed to assassinate the leadership of the loyalist UDA attending a meeting above Frizzell's fish shop on the Shankill Road, Belfast. Two IRA members disguised as deliverymen entered the shop carrying a bomb which detonated prematurely. Ten people were killed including one of the IRA bombers, a UDA member and eight Protestant civilians, with more than fifty people wounded. The family lived at 133 Forthriver Parade, Belfast, with two other children left parentless as a result of the explosion.

Trail 13 – Accidents

This trail is sponsored by Elizabeth and Ivan Towe, in memory of Elizabeth's brother Jackie Scott who is buried at P-971 and is featured below. This section features those killed as the result of an accident and includes, amongst others, victims of the Kegworth Air Disaster, as well as the Chinook helicopter crash on the Mull of Kintyre.

Arnold Clarke - D-150 - Clarke is commemorated at this grave as having 'died 1st Sept 1958 aged 14 years', whilst living at 10 Jonesboro Street, Belfast. Clarke was struck by a lorry in the Loopland area of the Castlereagh Road whilst riding his bicycle home after attending a prefects' meeting at Orangefield Boys High School, just as he was about to start his second year at the school. The Clarke family were members of Mountpottinger No 1 Corps of the Salvation Army, with Arnold's large funeral thronging the Castlereagh Road. The school then instigated the Arnold Clarke Memorial Cup, presented on an annual basis to the House gaining the highest points score for activities throughout the year. Additional information on Clarke's death is in a dedicated chapter of *Orangefield Remembered - A School in Belfast 1957-1990* produced after the school closed.

John Corbett Whiteside - E-861 - this headstone was erected 'In loving memory of our dear son John C. died 4th November 1961 result of a drowning accident' aged 25. A sheet metal worker living at 66 Solway Street, Belfast, Whiteside and a friend were hunting for ducks at Ballydorn Bay, Killinchy. Whilst attempting to retrieve a duck from the water using a canoe, the canoe overturned leading to Whiteside's death. Also buried in this grave is John's father Samuel Whiteside who was also living at 66 Solway Street at the time of his death in 28 January 1971 aged 64.

Thomas S. Hunter - F-101 - 'Dearly loved husband of Helen and darling daddy of Amanda and Kimberly died as the result of an accident at work 19th October 1965 aged 24 years'. Hunter, a steel erector employed by McLaughlin & Harvey, was working on an extension to Musgrave Park Hospital, Belfast when a manual lift which he had been dismantling fell 90 feet to the ground. Hunter was living at 113 Hornbeam Road, Dunmurry at the time of his death.

Anthony S Buchanan - U-1934 - 'Born 14th July 1943. Accidentally killed in Moab, Utah, U.S.A. 18th July 1967'. Moab is a city on the southern edge of Grand County in southeastern Utah in the western United States. Known for its dramatic scenery, Moab attracts many tourists annually, mostly visitors to the nearby Arches and Canyonlands national parks. The town is a popular base for mountain bikers who ride the extensive network of trails including the Slickrock Trail, and for off-roaders who come for the annual Moab Jeep Safari. I wonder if the death of Buchanan, whose home address was recorded as 3 Wallasey Park, Belfast and who was aged 24 when he died, was linked to either of these activities? Also buried in this plot, but not commemorated on the headstone, is Helen Weir Buchanan who was living at 32 Crosby Flats, Bangor when she died on 28 March 1985 aged 72.

Kenneth Watson - T-1092 - 'Precious memories of our dearly loved son L/Cpl Kenneth Watson R.C.T. [Royal Corps of Transport] died result of an accident in Germany on 25th May 1970 aged 22 years. Loved with a love beyond all telling, missed with a grief beyond all tears'. Watson's home address was 14 Malton Gardens, Belfast and he was aged 22 at the time of his death, and he was buried on 2 June 1970. Also buried in this grave is Alexander Watson who was living at 40 Lysander Park, Newtownards when he died on 24 June 1972 aged 49, and Dorothy Alice Watson who was living at 37 Beaufort Walk, Newtownards when she died on 30 July 1987 aged 62, both remembered on a plaque at the base of the headstone as 'Never for a moment are you far from our thoughts'.

Arthur Lyttle - T-929 - Lyttle is commemorated on this headstone as 'killed climbing at Glencoe 23rd Aug. 1970 aged 19 years' whilst registered as living at 32 Rathcoole Street, Belfast. Arthur's mother, a 'dear wife', Bertha Lyttle died within a month of her son, dying on 9

September 1970 aged 57, with his father Austin Lyttle dying on 31 December 2002 aged 89, both whilst also living at 32 Rathcoole Street.

Thomas G Neill - T-1416 - 'My dear husband Gdsm. [Guardsman] T.G. Neill died in Hong Kong as result of an accident 30th May 1971 aged 23 years'. Neill was buried on 10 June 1971, with his home address registered as 5 Egeria Street, Belfast. Also buried in this grave is James Boyd who died on 29 December 2000 aged 86, and Margaret Boyd who died on 22 November 2001 aged 85, both whilst also recorded as living at 5 Egeria Street.

Frank and Annie Annett - T-3419 - this headstone was erected 'in loving memory of our dear parents Frank and Annie killed 27th July 1973', with a plaque at the bottom of the headstone stating 'Treasured memories of a loving Wife & Mum Deep in our hearts You will always stay, Loved and remembered, Every day'. Frank and Annie were aged 69 and 67 respectively and were living at 6 Tavanagh Street, Belfast at the time of their deaths. The death notices for the Annetts in the Belfast Telegraph record that they died 'as a result of an accident in England', with the main notices from their sons Jim and Frankie and daughters Vi, Anne, Winnie and Rita, as well as from the 'Employees of the Monarch Laundry'. The Monarch Laundry, at the corner of the Donegall Road and Monarch Street, opened in 1904 with a red brick chimney the only reminder of the demolished wash house. There are plans to build 53 apartments on the site, which is now largely waste ground overlooking the busy Westlink.

George Desmond (Dessie) Hunt - T-3813 - 'killed in the Paris air disaster 3rd March 1974'. Turkish Airlines Flight 981 was a scheduled flight from Istanbul Yesilköy airport to London Heathrow airport, with an intermediate stop at Orly airport in Paris. The crash occurred when an incorrectly secured cargo door at the rear of the plane burst open and broke off, causing an explosive decompression that severed critical cables necessary to control the aircraft, killing all 346 people on board. At the time, Flight 981 - known as the Ermenonville air disaster - was the deadliest plane crash in aviation history, and remains the deadliest single-aircraft accident without survivors. Hunt was living at 27 Edgcumbe Gardens, Belfast and was aged 47 at the time of his death, and was buried on 28 May 1974. A Scout logo at the top of the headstone indicates that Dessie was a Scout leader and he was, in fact, friendly with Clive Scoular who proof-read this publication and the two were both active in the Scouting movement. Also buried in this plot is Desmond's wife Ramona who 'died 16th August 2013'.

William (Ben) Beattie - U-425 - 'died result of a climbing accident on Nanda Devi, Himalayas 15th September 1978'. Nanda Devi is the second highest mountain in India after Kangchenjunga and the highest located entirely within the country. It is the 23rd highest peak in the world. It was considered the highest mountain in the world before computations in 1808 proved Dhaulagiri to be higher. Beattie is only commemorated on this headstone, so I would imagine that, sadly, his body was perhaps never recovered. Interred in this plot is Ben's father William Beattie who was living at 15 Legmore Street, Belfast when he died on 6 February 1966 aged 51, and his mother Eileen Beattie who was living at 52 Ligoniel Road, Belfast when she died on 14 April 2000 aged 79. The base of this headstone reads 'Deeply loved and sorely missed'.

Brian Wilson - U-2161 - 'died 15th March 1979 aged 18½ result of an accident. Boy rider to the end'. On this headstone is an image of a motorbike, with a helmet sitting on the seat of the bike. Brian was living at 9 Ballymacruise Drive, Millisle at the time of his death, with his death notices including one from his friends 'George, Ernie and Jeff. A smiling face, a heart of gold, no better friend this world could hold'. Also interred in this plot is Brian's grandmother 'dearly loved wife of the late George Birney', Henrietta Birney who was living at 71 Disraeli Street, Belfast when she died on 10 July 1968 aged 68. The base of the headstone reads 'where your treasure is there shall your heart be also'.

Moloney - R-3444 - 'Denis and Pearl 8th January 1989 "A devoted couple, kind and gentle, they did everything together. They were always to be seen together in life and their bodies were found together in death. They died hand in hand." (Homily). We will keep in our hearts the love of the past,

for there it was planted forever to last. Love does not come to an end. Denis and Maria'. The Moloneys were killed in the Kegworth Air Disaster which occurred when a British Midland Boeing 737-400 crashed onto a motorway embankment while attempting to make an emergency landing at East Midlands Airport. The aircraft was on a scheduled flight from London Heathrow airport to Belfast International airport when a fan-blade broke in the left engine, disrupting the air conditioning and filling the cabin with smoke. The pilots mistakenly shut down the functioning of the aircraft's two engines and selected full thrust from the malfunctioning one, causing it to catch fire. Of the 126 people aboard, 47 died (including the Moloneys, and John and Karin Campbell mentioned in Trail 10 in this publication), 74 sustained serious injuries, and five suffered minor injuries. All eight members of the crew survived the accident.

Siobhann Kennedy - R-2640 - this unusual, faded headstone commemorates 'our only daughter Siobhann Maria Kennedy Pytharas killed tragically 26th May 1989 aged 21 years', with the location of death listed as 'Queens University'. Siobhann, who was from London and whose father was of Greek origin, was a student at the university when she was struck by a car whilst cycling along the Malone Road, Belfast. Eddie McCrudden, a member of a top local showband, the Smirnoff Jazz Band, was charged with causing Siobhann's death. A faded photo of Siobhann features on the headstone, with the base of the headstone reading 'a banquet is prepared and your cup runneth over Your head is anointed with oil'.

Bate - R-3962 - this headstone was erected 'in loving memory of our dear parents John, aged 72 years, and Molly [Matilda Elizabeth], aged 71 years Died as they lived together as the result of a freak accident on 20 May 1992', whilst living at 12 Newry Street, Belfast. John and Molly died when a young pigeon died and blocked the chimney of their Newry Street house, with the couple found dead in front of their glass-fronted fire. My Granda Craig's sister Irene Crothers also died as a result of an incident involving a glass-fronted fire, and was buried in the grave beside my Granny and Granda - R-3294 - dying on 29 September 1996 aged 78, having been predeceased by her husband William (Billy) who died on 23 November 1990 aged 73, both whilst registered as living at 6 Lichfield Avenue, Belfast.

Jonathan Paul Tapper - P-444 - this military headstone commemorates 'Flight Lieutenant Jonathan Paul Tapper [who died] 2nd June 1994 aged 28 Mull of Kintyre'. Tapper died when a Royal Air Force Chinook helicopter crashed in foggy conditions on the Mull of Kintyre leading to the deaths of all 25 passengers and four crew on board. Among the passengers were almost all the United Kingdom's senior Northern Ireland intelligence experts, and the accident is the RAF's worst peacetime disaster. A stone cairn near the crash site commemorates this disaster.

John (Jackie) Forsythe Scott - P-971 - Jackie, the husband of Karen, and father of Catherine, Megan and Jonathan, was tragically killed in an early morning accident on the M62 in Manchester on 6 June 1994. Jackie was travelling in a taxi on his way to Manchester airport when

an articulated lorry careered into the path of the taxi killing Jackie and seriously injuring the taxi driver. Jackie, 'a dearly loved husband and father', was living in Whitefield, Greater Manchester at the time of his death aged 55, and was buried on 15 June 1994.

Paine - R-3450 - Stephen (49), Sile (42) Thomas (13) Cara (11) and Sophia (4) are recorded at the bottom of this headstone as having 'died in a plane crash 21st April 1995', whilst all recorded as living at 2009 Myrtle Bend Drive, Germantown, Tennessee, and were interred more than six months later on 30 December 1995. Also buried in this grave is Sile's father Thomas Joseph McCoy who died on 13 May 1989 aged 80, and her mother Margaret who died on 10 June 2017 aged 97.

Nicholas (Nicky) Maguire - S-525 (memorial tree) - 'Oct 69 - Feb 00 B.A. (Hons) P.G.C.E beloved son of Joyce and Tom 'to teach is to touch a life forever'. Nicky was a lifelong friend of mine having been born in the same hospital in October 1969, and attended the same schools and university, dying tragically in a house fire in Lisbellaw whilst a teacher in Lisnaskea High School. A plaque beside Nicky's memorial tree states 'Suddenly you were gone from all the lives you left your mark upon./I tried to believe, but you know it's no good./This is something that cannot be understood./I feel the way you would; I remember'. Tragically Nicky's father predeceased him with 'Tom [a] devoted husband, father and loyal friend' dying in May 1999, aged 61, with his heartbroken mother Joyce, a 'much loved wife, mother and companion, a lady worthy of remembrance, our lives have been touched by the hand of true friendship', dying in March 2013 aged 69.

Christian - Y-648/9 - Jonathan and Jacob Christian drowned whilst fishing from the shore of Lough Keel, county Donegal, on 18 June 2021. 17-year-old Jacob went into the water to retrieve something he had dropped but as he got further and further out, his father Jonathan (53) jumped in to rescue him, but sadly both drowned. Both father and son were brought up in Douglas, Isle of Man, with Jonathan involved in many enterprises, including Heritage Lane which sold miniature cottages worldwide, and was also the proprietor of Arcadia Stationery and The Corporate Centre in Strand Street. Jonathan and his wife Eileen married in 2001 and their eight children were members of The Church of Jesus Christ of Latter-day Saints on Woodbourne Road, Douglas from where their funeral service was conducted.

Marc and Wayne Wallace - W-442 - this black double headstone was erected to commemorate 'Precious memories of our beloved twin sons Marc and Wayne died 15th April 2006 aged 19 years', with the base of the headstone stating 'Together forever in God's keeping'. The Wallace twins were both killed when a car in which they were travelling - driven by David Campbell, buried opposite at W-387 - crashed on the Ballygowan Road, almost opposite the main entrance to Roselawn. The 16-year-old son of the minister who officiated at the twins' funeral service in St Columba's Church, Belfast, Archdeacon Gregor McCamley, had been left permanently brain damaged from a previous road traffic accident. The Wallace twins lived at 28 Sandhill Park, Belfast, with Campbell living at 1 Lewis Court, Belfast when he died aged 18.

Gareth James Keys - W-1026 – a 27-year-old service engineer, Keys died after being injured while checking a hydraulic platform which toppled over crushing his spine and chest at his workplace in Highway Plant Co Ltd, Dunmurry on 16 May 2008. A father of two and a former student of Royal Belfast Academical Institution, Keys previously served his engineering apprenticeship at Harland and Wolff. His impressive headstone, with the representation of a lion on top of it, above a red hand and shamrock with the words 'Holy bible', and flanked by the words 'One true God' and 'One true people' states: 'Here lies a loyal Anglo-Saxon-Celt Gareth James Keys. Son of William & Jennifer, Father of Joel & Sharon. Born 10th Jan 1981, present with Our LORD from 16th May 2008', followed by lots more text.

Trail 14 – Celtic Cousins

This trail is sponsored by Lyndesay McLea, a previous supporter of my publications.

This section features 21 headstones that mention either Ireland or Scotland, recognising our close links both across the border and 'the sheugh'.

Madeline Crozier Lambe - D-490 - Dundee - 'widow of the late Alexander Lambe of Dundee, Scotland' who was living at 41 Tower Street, Belfast when she died on 5 July 1959 aged 72. Also buried in this plot is Margaret Moore who was registered as living at 42 Tower Street when she died on 21 June 1963 aged 65, and Martha Moore who died at Enler House, Dundonald on 22 May 1984 aged 85, with the latter not recorded on the headstone.

Ralph Vincent Larmour - E-398 - Aberdeen - 'Rev R V Larmour died 21st July 1961' aged 42 whilst living at 153 Clifton Road, Aberdeen. The only reference that I can find to Rev. Larmour refers to an essay he produced entitled 'Truth and Truthfulness'. Also buried in this grave is Rev. Larmour's father Ernest Wesley Larmour 'who died 21st April 1962 aged 71 years' whilst living at 32 Cliftonpark Avenue, Belfast, and his mother Florence Lamour who was living at Clifton House, North Queen Street, Belfast when she died on 11 August 1972 aged 83. The base of this headstone states 'Blessed are the pure in heart for they shall see God'.

Robert James Armstrong - E-824 - Stranraer - 'eldest son of William and Agnes Armstrong [of] Stranraer, Scotland died 12th October 1961', aged 68 whilst living at 264 Ravenhill Avenue, Belfast. Armstrong appears to be the only committal in this plot. For a decade my Dad had a Stranraer season ticket, and used to travel over to Stair Park every fortnight to see the Blues, so I always think of this, and the annual 'boys day out' with my Dad and brother, when I hear the town mentioned.

Matilda Thompson - D-1978 - Raphoe, county Donegal - 'in loving memory of Matilda widow of Robert Thompson of Raphoe Died 21st November 1963' aged 86 whilst living at 143 Sicily Park, Finaghy. Also buried in this plot are four daughters of the couple; Mabel Frances Henderson Thompson was also living at 143 Sicily Park when she died on 21 August 1964 aged 57, Martha Adeline Thompson who was living at 202c Lisburn Road, Finaghy when she died on 19 March 1969 aged 69, Anna V. M. Gillan who was living 19 The Glen, Worthing, Sussex when she died on 28 March 1988 aged 76, and Katherine Elliott who died on 15 April 1990 aged 87, whilst also living at 19 The Glen.

Marguerite Frances (Daisy) Rowe - F-238 - Greystones, county Wicklow - this headstone states that Daisy 'died at Greystones 31st August 1965' aged 58, whilst registered as living at 33 Kerrsland Crescent, Belfast, with the headstone also featuring an image of daisies. Also buried in this plot is Daisy's sister Anne Mary Rowe who was living at Hawthorn Residential Home, Hawthornden Road, Belfast when she died on 29 July 1996 aged 93. The base of the headstone states 'there by his love o'ershaded.....those angel faces smile'.

Allen Simpson - S-1353 - Cambuslang - 'Born 20th September 1955. Murdered 3rd April 1975 by the enemies of Ulster' aged 19. Simpson was a member of the Ulster Defence Association (UDA), and was killed by a non-specific Republican group at his home at 92 Highfield Drive, Belfast. A plaque at the base of the headstone is 'in memory of Allen Simpson died 3rd April 1975 aged 19 years from friends and loyalists, Cambuslang'. This grave also contains William John Simpson who was living at 7 Braeside Avenue, Newtownabbey when he died on 8 June 1994 aged 68.

Louisa Isobel (Loubell) McManus - S-1796 - Arva, county Cavan - 'born 18th September 1918 Arva, Co. Cavan', Loubell moved from Lakeview House, Brankill, Arva to Belfast with her family in 1926, and became an Auxillary Nurse at the Royal Victoria Hospital during World War Two. Also commemorated on this headstone is her husband, John (Johnny) George McManus 'born Mohill, Co. Leitrim

1908'. Johnny, and his brother Tom mentioned in the entry below, came from Mohill, county Leitrim living initially in 105 Rathmore Street, Belfast. Johnny was a painter in Harland & Wolff and part-time B Special, joining the Irish Guards on 10 February 1940, serving with the  1st and then 2nd Batallions before he was demobbed in July 1945, and becoming full-time with the Royal Ulster Constabulary. Loubell and Johnny married on 21 March 1942 in St. Donards church. Johnny McManus was cousin of a grandmother of Stewart McCracken (sponsor of two chapters in this book) and the two were firm friends as well. Johnny died on 15 May 1977 aged 68, with Loubell dying on 21 May 2007 aged 88 both whilst living at 20 Flush Green, Belfast, with the base of the headstone stating 'At Rest'.

Thomas (Tom) William McManus - U-1784 - Mohill, county Leitrim - A joiner by trade, Tom then worked for McCann's pubs, becoming a Director of the company when it became known as Braithwaite McCann. Good friends with the boss, Colonel Alexander Hamilton McCann of Warren Road, Donaghadee, Tom was living at 21 Knocklofty Park, Belfast when he died on 10 April 1967 aged 59, with his wife Annie E McManus living at 249 Donaghadee Road, Bangor when she died on 17 October 1977 aged 68. Like his brother Johnny - featured in the previous entry - Tom hailed from the town of Mohill, county Leitrim. Tom was a cousin of Stewart McCracken's grandmother, whilst a daughter of Tom and Annie's is 'Happy' Parker who is married to the Rev Brian Parker, and their son is Rev. Canon Michael Parker, rector of Carnalea Parish Church, with the Parkers known to my Mum and Dad. Mohill is closely associated with Turlough Carolan, the blind harpist, who lived in the town after his marriage.

Douglas Hyde, the first president of Ireland, whose family originated from the town, also spent some of his childhood there, whilst Matthew Sadlier, a 20-year-old from Mohill, did not survive *RMS Titanic*'s sinking in 1912.

William James Ferguson - S-1764 - Scotland - '(ex R.U.R.) died 5th Feb. 1981' aged 81 whilst living at 11 Abetta Parade, Belfast. Plaques at the base of the headstone, each featuring the Scottish saltire, commemorate 'Granda forever in our thoughts' and 'Dad always loved and missed'. Ferguson was predeceased by his wife Sarah Elizabeth (Lily) Ferguson who died on 22 February 1977 aged 79 whilst living at 40 Avoniel Road, Belfast. Also commemorated at this grave is a son 'Thomas G (Ex R.M) [Royal Marines] interred in Victoria, Canada', and another son Robert Gordon Ferguson who died on 31 August 2009 aged 69 whilst living at 30 Mayflower Street, Belfast.

Victor Hollinger - V-1568 - Caddagh, county Monaghan - 'everlasting memories of Victor died 17 April 1981. Born February 1911 Caddagh Ballybay'. Victor was registered as living at 145 Cavehill Road, Belfast when he died aged 70. Caddagh is a townland between Monaghan and Ballybay in county Monaghan. A company called King Hollinger still operate in the Ballybay area, so I would suggest that Victor is related to these Hollingers.

Thomas Geddis - V-2299 - Scotland - 'Cherished memories of a dearly loved husband and father Pipe Major Thomas Geddis died 7th May 1983' aged 54 whilst living at 61 St Judes Parade, Belfast. This headstone also contains the logo of R.S.P.B.A. (Royal Scottish Pipe Band Association) and a coat of arms by the Lord Lyon King of Arms in Edinburgh, with the motto 'Ceol na h-Alba' (Music of Scotland).

Samuel Kennedy - V-2303 - Dalbeattie - 'died in Scotland 3rd June 1983' aged 57. The location of death is given as '12 Doon Valley Caravan Park', Dalbeattie. Also buried in this plot is 'a beloved wife, mum, nanny and great granny Violet (Vi) died 24th October 2000 aged 76', living at 3d Ardfarn Close, Newtownabbey at the time of her death.

Elspeth (Hen) Andrews - Y-1501 - Scotland - 'A much loved wife, mother and grandmother Died 17th March 2017'. Representations of a set of bagpipes and an accordion are on this headstone, suggesting an interest in Scottish music, with the words 'Unchained melody' either side of musical notes at the base of the headstone.

Mary Elizabeth Waterhouse, M.A. - D-598 - Dublin - this headstone commemorates the 'elder daughter of Sir Robert Woods of Dublin 1896-1980' who died on 13 November 1980 aged 84 whilst registered as living at 6 Knockdene Park, Belfast. Woods was born in Tullamore, county Offaly in 1865, and attended Wesley College, Dublin and Trinity College, Dublin as well as studying in Vienna, before graduating in medicine in 1889. In 1910-11, he became President of the Royal College of Surgeons in Ireland. Professor of Laryngology and Otology at Trinity College, and knighted in 1913, Woods was also MP for Dublin University between 1918 and 1922. This headstone also commemorates Mary's husband 'Gilbert Waterhouse, M.A. Litt. D. elder son of Harold Waterhouse of Lancashire 1888-1977', a Professor of German at Queen's University, Belfast from 1933 until 1953, who was living at 92 Malone Road, Belfast when he died on 25 July 1977 aged 89.

Florence Evaline Jones - T-2388 - Blackrock, Dublin - 'died 17th November 1998. Interred in Dean's Grange Cemetery Blackrock', Dublin. Interred in this grave is Florence's husband Tom Gilliland Jones who died on 19 October 1973 aged 77 whilst living at 24 Blenheim Park, Carryduff. Deansgrange Cemetery is situated in the suburban area of Deansgrange in the Dún Laoghaire–Rathdown part of the former county Dublin. Since it first opened in 1865, over 150,000 people have been buried there and, together with Glasnevin and Mount Jerome, is one of the largest cemeteries in the Dublin area, occupying 70 acres.

Denis Noonan - W-466 - Camphire, county Waterford - 'a very dear loving and kind husband, father and grandfather Born Camphire, Co. Waterford 21 February 1921 Died Belfast 8 February 2007' aged 85. Noonan was living at 14 Abbey Park, Belfast when he died. Also buried in this grave is 'Mary his beloved wife and a devoted mother, grandmother and great grandmother Born Workington England 10 January 1923 Died Belfast 19 October 2016', with the base of the headstone stating 'St Martin de Porres Pray For Us'.

Elizabeth (Liz) Reid - W-1156 - County Donegal - 'Born: 14 May 1959 Died: 21 March 2008 Missed ... like a heartbeat in Life. Loved like a summer in Donegal'. Elizabeth was recorded as living at 54 Marlborough Park Central, Belfast when she died on 21 March 2008 aged 48.

Carolyn Murray - R-2419 - County Wexford - 'our dear sister Carolyn died 14th July 2008 aged 48 years. Ashes scattered at Hook lighthouse. Forever missed by Anne, Samuel, David and Carolyn's five children David, Darren, Aaron, Rebecca and Gemma'. The Hook Lighthouse, also known as Hook Head Lighthouse, is at the tip of the Hook Peninsula in county Wexford. The second oldest operating lighthouse in the world, it marks the eastern entrance to Waterford harbour, with the current structure existing for 849 years as of 2021. Commemorated on this headstone is 'Our dear mother Elizabeth died

19th January 1967 aged 37 years (C409 City Cemetery)' - actually plot C1-409 in the Glenalina section of the City Cemetery - who was living at 24 Highfield Drive, Belfast when she died. The only interment in this plot is 'our dear father Samuel [Murray] died 12th September 1988 aged 62 years', whilst recorded as living at 34 Ramore Park, Finaghy.

Sergeant Sean Conor Binnie - W-1886 - Scotland - this military headstone commemorates Sergeant Binnie 'The Royal Regiment of Scotland 7 May 2009 aged 22', with the base of the grave commemorating a 'Loving husband and son, our true hero, God be with you, Till we meet again'. A Scottish flag has also been placed on this grave, along with several plaques. Binnie had been part of a battlegroup mentoring the Afghan National Army when he was shot by Taliban insurgents while carrying out a routine patrol in the Musa Qal'eh region. Sergeant Binnie was registered as living at 1 Pearl Court, Woodstock Road, Belfast when he died, and was buried on 22 May 2009.

Whillans - W-1215 - Jedburgh - 'Precious memories of George Stewart [Whillans] 21st May 1935 - 23rd May 2009 A much loved Husband, Dad and Gaffie' who was living at 15 Harland Park, Belfast at the time of his death aged 74. Also buried in this grave is 'his beloved wife Edith nee Buchanan 23rd May 1936 - 15th November 2016 Our wonderful Mum and Grannie'. Beneath a Scottish saltire at the top of the headstone are the words 'Whillans Jedburgh, Scotland', with the base of the headstone reading 'Never more than a thought away. Loved and remembered every day'. Jedburgh is a town and former royal burgh in the Scottish Borders, ten miles from the English border and, in sporting terms, is best known as the home town of scrum-halves, Roy Laidlaw and Gary Armstrong, and former Scotland rugby team captain Greig Laidlaw.

James Cook - Y-2126 - Lochaber - this headstone features a logo (presumably of the Lord of Lochaber) and commemorates the 'Laird of Lochaber 27th August 1946 27th April 2016'. The titles 'Laird, Lord or Lady of Glencoe and Lochaber' are trademarked Highland titles available for purchase online. The base of the headstone also contains the words 'Wanderin' star' with the image of a horse.

Trail 15 – Not From This Parish

This trail is sponsored by my good friend Eric Woods, who is presently working on a tome about the Sirocco Works and the remarkable Samuel Cleland Davidson, with Eric's sponsorship of this trail appropriate as he spent many years of his life working overseas.

This section looks at the graves of people seemingly not originally from this neck of the woods.

Dr Louis Kanitz - D-2057 - 'in loving memory of Dr Louis Kanitz 1893 -1961', with Dr Kanitz registered as living at 17 Evelyn Gardens, Belfast when he died on 7 August 1961 aged 68, and was buried on 4 December 1961. Also buried in this plot, but not commemorated on the headstone, is Mary Kanitz who died on 9 May 1979.

Ludmilla Polz - U-731 - 'a devoted wife and loving mother 1st Dec. 1889 - 18th June 1967' dying aged 78, whilst registered as living at 21 Wynchurch Walk, Belfast. This headstone also remembers 'her dear husband Johann 1st Nov. 1889 - 25th Nov. 1970' who died aged 81 whilst living at 13 Tennyson Avenue, Bangor, and their son Maxi William Polz '3rd Oct 1931 - 15th Sept 1994 loving father and grandfather' who died aged 62 whilst living at 13 Manor Park, Bangor, with the base of this headstone stating 'Sweet repose'.

Toan - U-1083 - the base of this headstone states 'Of Hugenot descent', with the grave containing Henry Toan who died on 14 May 1969 aged 75 whilst living at 79 Hunter Street, Belfast, Thomas Toan who was living at 195 Clarawood Park, Belfast when he died on 20 June 1969 aged 45, and Frances Toan who was also living at 79 Hunter Street when he died on 27 March 1982 aged 78.

Leopold Fritsch - T-2106 - 'Died on 28th January 1973. He loved and was being loved', with the base of the headstone reading 'Na Scledanou' which translates from Czech as 'Goodbye'. Fritsch was living at Vantier Strasse, 73 Dusseldorf when he died aged 65, and was

buried on 5 February 1973. Also buried in this plot, but not commemorated at the grave in any way, is Elsie Fritsch who was living at the same address when she died on 5 January 1983 aged 64, and was buried on 11 January 1983.

George William Shummacher, OBE - T-2917 - Shummacher was living at 143 Sandown Road, Belfast when he died on 17 November 1973 aged 83, with his wife Ethel Shummacher dying on 1 August 1979 aged 89. Also buried in this plot is Betty Smart who was living at 43 Norwood Avenue, Belfast when she died on 7 August 1992 aged 73, and her husband Canon Sydney Smart who was living at 49 Ballylenaghan Park, Belfast when he died on 15 May 2006 aged 90. Canon Smart was in the same class as my Granda McCabe at school and, in retirement, was very involved in St Elizabeth's church when I was growing up. A gentleman.

Cesira Traversari - V-618 - Cesira (née Meli) was living at 40 Downshire Road, Belfast when she died on 15 July 1980 aged 66. Also buried in this grave is 'her beloved husband' Dominic Traversari who died on 2 July 1989 aged 76, also living at 40 Downshire Road when he died.

Ghulam Mohummed - C-1221 - 'Muslim Born 1909 Died 1983 Dear husband of Rehmat Bibi and father of Shehnaz Gulnaz'. Mohummed was living at 15 Casaeldona Gardens, Belfast when he died on 5 August 1983 aged 73. Mohummed's death predates the creation of the separate Muslim plot, in part of section W, as mentioned elsewhere in this publication on a number of occasions.

De Croock - S-4130 - Archier Louis (John) De Croock died on 14 January 1984 aged 63, with his wife Sarah (Sadie) De Croock dying on 20 December 1999 aged 75, both whilst living at 51 Springfield Parade, Belfast. The base of the states "Forever In Our Thoughts".

Ruston Zarea Aliabadi - P-71 - 'passed on 27th March 1994', with the base of the headstone stating '"Death conferreth the gift of everlasting life" Ba'hai scripture'. Aliabadi was registered as living at 20 Rugby Avenue, Belfast when he died aged 79. The Bahá'í Faith is a new religion teaching the essential worth of all religions and the unity of all people. Established by Bahá'u'lláh in the 19th century, it initially grew in Persia and parts of the Middle East, where it has faced ongoing persecution since its inception.

Margarita Kennedy - P-468 - 'in loving memory of Margarita "Momo" nee Hoestra 3 Nov. 1921 - 10 Apr 1996' who died aged 74 whilst living at 29 Tweskard Park, Belfast. A plaque on this headstone states 'Momo our very dear Mum. Intelligent and industrious of Nordic origin and Louisiana upbringing who cherished and respected all life and recognised what was truly important. You taught us by your loving example. Now resting in love eternal'. Also buried in this plot, but not commemorated on this headstone in any way, is Edward Kennedy who died on 9 June 2002 aged 82 whilst also living at 29 Tweskard Park.

Beman Khosravinezhad - R-3818 - this headstone commemorates 'a loving husband and father Iran 1933 - 18th August 2006', with the base of the headstone stating '"Let your vision be world embracing" Ba'hai writings'. Khosravinezhad was living at 8 Kingsway Park, Belfast when he died aged 72. Also buried in this grave is his mother-in-law Violet Patrick, a 'dear gentle mother' and 'wife of Campbell died 13th June 1992 aged 89', whilst living at 45 Knockvale Park, Belfast.

Solomon Oshagbemi - W-158 - '22nd February 1977 - 30th March 2008', Oshagbemi was living at 8 Chesham Gardens, Belfast at the time of his death, and was buried on 11 April 2008. Also buried in this plot is 'Titus Adekunle Oshagbemi 30th September 1948 - 15th June 2018', with the base of the headstone stating 'Safe in the arms of Jesus'.

Anneliese Gisela Lavery - W-881 - 'nee Lehmann. Beloved wife, mother and grandmother. Born Duisburg, Germany 12th May 1939 Died 24th March 2008' aged 68, whilst living at 21 Broomhill Park, Belfast, with the base of the headstone stating 'Eternity must be mine, with peace and happiness I depart'.

Adolf Karel August Bulens Twibill - R-3338 - 'Died 25th December 2008, aged 87'. Also interred in this grave is Robert Twibill who died on 25 March 1993 aged 81, and Annie Twibill who died on 24 September 1997 aged 86, all three recorded as living at 26 Hawthornden Drive, Belfast at the time of their deaths.

Marcin Abramczyk - W-2964 - 'in loving memory of my beloved husband Born 28-2-1983 - Died 26-3-2015 Co nas spotkato was nie ominie. My jestesmy W Domu A Ny N goscinie', which appears to translate from Polish as 'What will happen to us will not pass by. We are at home and guests are welcome'. This headstone also features a photo of a smiling Abramczyk, who was aged 32 when he died.

Mina Emamli-Mahdi - Y-1503 - the top of this headstone features a flower along with the words 'Mina Mahdi', along with the number 9 surrounded by a nine-sided star, and the following inscription: 'O Son Of Spirit! Burst thy cage asunder, and even as the phoenix of love soar into the firmament of holiness...- Baha 'u' lla. Mina Emamli-Mahdi April 1923 - 7 April 2017'. Nearby at Plot Y-1683 is a headstone

commemorating 'Narain Assudamall Sherwani 1st July 1936 - 6th August 2018. Loving father and grandfather. Unique in mind and soul, Forever in our hearts. A pioneer of the Baha'i Faith "The earth is but one country, and mankind its citizens". Baha'u'llah'.

Bialecki - Y-2142 - 'in loving memory of Janusz (Jasiek) 23 April 1976 - 20 June 2017 na zawsze pozostaniesz w naszych sercach' which, translated from Polish, means 'you will always remain in our hearts'. People tend to think that the migration of a significant number of folks from Poland is a new thing, forgetting, for example, the many Polish airmen who died fighting for the Allied cause during the Second World War. A number of such airmen are buried in Milltown Cemetery, Belfast, with three others - Lieutenant Henryk Komenda, Sergeant Henryk Andrzej Flegier and Wing Commander W. E. Heller - also buried in neighbouring graves in Movilla Cemetery, Newtownards and featuring in the relevant chapter in my *2020* book.

Offodum - Y-1533 - 'Jude Chukwuemeka a much loved and loving partner, father, son, brother and friend 28th October 1959 - 28th February 2018. His inspiration lives on', whilst the base of this headstone contains the words 'I did it my way'. The same sentiment - "I did it my way" - is also at the base of the headstone of Ernie Watson, buried at D-820, who died on 3 May 2017.

Solinas - Y-1532 - 'in loving memory of my dearest father Teodoro Raphael Pascal (Dorino) a beloved grandfather, brother and uncle. Born 6th September 1948 Departed this earth 7th March 2018'. The top of this headstone features a carved representation of the last supper, whilst the base states 'You will always live in our hearts and walk through the memories of our minds'.

Dragana Mahaffy - Y-2731 - this headstone was erected 'in loving memory of my devoted wife Dragana 18th August 1972 - 25th December 2018. Почивај у миру љубави моја' which translates from Serbian as 'Rest in peace my love'. I was talking to Dragana's husband, Gordon, near her headstone, and he informed me that his wife was an investigative journalist and author in Serbia, specialising in the Serbian Mafia, before moving to Northern Ireland, to quote Gordon, 'from Belgrade to Belfast'. Tragically Dragana developed cancer shortly after moving to Belfast, dying unexpectedly from a blood clot on Christmas Day 2018 aged 46.

Muhammad Irfan Farooque - W-4052 - '23/03/1984 - 15/03/2019 You will always remain in our hearts and prayers. A loving father, husband, son and brother. Proud doctor and Chairman of KMDC Alumni Association', an association for the Karachi Medical and Dental College.

Trail 16 – Chinese Community

Stewart McCracken has kindly sponsored this section, along with Chapter 12.

This trail features folks who I think are of Chinese origin, and I am indebted to Min Shen for his translation skills in this section.

Teh - U-986 - this headstone commemorates 'Pal-Oon Father 6 Sept. 1910 - 11 July 1969' aged 60, 'Leng Leng Daughter 7 Aug. 1934 - 6 Nov. 1996' aged 62 and 'Cheng Hui Mother 26 Jan. 1912 - 18 April 1998' aged 86. All three were living at 18 Drumart Walk, Belvoir at the times of their deaths, with the base of the headstone stating 'Mortal must put on immortality'. Commemorated on a plaque at the base of the headstone is 'Teh Kean Chong Son 17.7.1941 - 19.7.2014 In paradise with the Lord'.

You Fan - S-3963 - 'a dear husband and father ... died 19th November 1982' aged 63 whilst living at 63 Wellesley Avenue, Belfast. Also interred in this grave is 'a devoted wife and mother Yuk Ying Fan died 25th July 1996' aged 74 whilst living at 41 Montgomery Road, Sheffield.

Ki Tei Chiang - R-2463 - Chiang, 'a devoted wife and mother', was living at 31 Connsbrook Park, Belfast when she died on 2 May 1989 aged 50, whilst also interred in this grave is a 'loving father Sai Chak Died 4th March 2017'.

Yau - P-195 - at the bottom right of this headstone are the words in English 'born 7th December 1927 Died 22nd April 1994', with Yau living at 2 Enler Gardens, Comber at the time of her death. The four accompanying columns in Chinese state 'From Hong Kong, Sha Tau Kok, [village name] Sheung Tam Shui Hang', 'Family Yau Of Lee Kwun Doi's Tomb', 'Erected by husband Yau Lam Choi and sons & grandchildren', and '22nd April 1994'.

Kam On Wong - P-202 - 'in memory of our loving son Kam On died 5 August 1994 aged 20 years' whilst registered as living at 60 Lower Windsor Avenue, Belfast. A photo of a smiling On, in a school uniform, adorns this grave.

Bong Chan - P-4038 - this headstone commemorates a 'dear husband died 26th November 1998 aged 65 years', whilst living at 10 Cathedral Row, Armagh. The base of the headstone states "Always in our hearts", with an Oriental-looking dwarf with a watering can placed at the bottom of the headstone.

Wan Nee Kiu Mo - P-1987 - 1990 - the text on this headstone states 'In loving memory of Mo Wan Nee Kiu a beloved wife mother and grandmother. Born 2nd May 1911 Died 28th Feb. 1999' aged 87 whilst registered as living at 30 Trossachs Drive, Belfast.

Lin Kin Lau - P-1991 - a photo of Mrs Lau features on this headstone which was erected 'in loving memory of a dear mother and grandmother died 9th May 1999' aged 63 whilst registered as living at 18 Loopland Grove, Belfast. The Lau family appear to also own the neighboiring plot P-1992, whilst the next plot P-1993 was erected 'in loving memory of Tai Wayne (Kenny) [Lau] 6th August 1981 13th March 2001', with Kenny aged 18 when he died whilst also registered as living at 18 Loopland Grove.

Kwai Ho Yu - P-2991 - 'Born 11th July 1920 Died 5th April 2003 loved and deeply missed by Man Hau, Suet Chow, Man Fung, Suet Chun, Siu To, Yuk Chi, Sin Fan, Hoi Ling'. This headstone also states 'John 11 Verse 25 Jesus Said Unto Her: "I am the resurrection and the life, he that believeth in me, though he were dead yet shall live"'. Yu was living at 3 Baronscourt Heights, Carryduff, and was aged 84 when she died.

Yee Yau Yuan - P-3407 - this grey headstone with gold lettering includes inscriptions stating 'Born on 2nd Mar 1932 Died on 14th Feb 2004 Mr Yuan ErYou's Tomb From Xiao MeiSha Town, Bao An City Erected By Biqi, Jianwei, Jianming'. Yuan was living at 39 Lakeside Drive, Belfast when he died aged 71.

Jun Wang - W-363 - '31st Oct. 1965 - 15th March 2005 In everlasting memory of our dear friend', with Wang living at 27 Hampton Drive, Belfast when they died, and was buried on 24 April 2006.

Loi Yau - W-132 - the only line of English on this headstone states 'In loving memory of a dear husband and father', with Yau living at 17 Castlehill, Comber when he died on 8 September 2005 aged 72. The Chinese writing in multiple columns states 'from Hong Kong, Sha Tau Kok, Sheung Tam Shui Hang. Yau Loi The Grandfather Fu Lau's Tomb. Born 24th July 1933 Died on 8th September 2005. Erected by remaining Wife Yau Wong Wai Doi and sons & daughters', with his sons listed as 'Yau Kok Leung, Yau Kok Leung, Yau Kok Loong, Yau Kok Hung and Yau Kok Yip and daughter Yau Shui Ling'. The final couple of columns acknowledge his 'grandson Yau Chin Hing and granddaughters Yau Chin Er and Yau Chin Mei'.

Ye Wan Mo - W-899 - 'Beloved wife of Wu Kie and dear mother of Jonathan 11th October 1968 - 11th June 2007', Mo was living at 9 Norton Drive, Belfast at the time of her death. Her headstone, which features her photo, also states 'If I could have a lifetime wish a dream that would come true, I'd pray to God with all my heart for yesterday and you. A thousand words can't bring you back I know because I've tried And neither will a million tears I know because I've cried. You left behind a broken heart and happy memories too I never wanted memories .... I only wanted you'.

Chung Wong Ying - W-822 - this headstone contains not a word of English, but translates as follows. Below the words Rest In Peace, the middle column states Chung Wong Ying's Tomb, with the column to the right stating Ying's birth date 26th August 1944, with the left column stating Died On 22nd November 2007.

Lo Fat (Tony) Cheung - W-1728 - the base of the headstone states 'In memory of a loving husband and devoted father 14th September 1959 - 5th December 2007', with Cheung living at 10 Dunkeld Road, Bangor when he died. The four columns of writing translate as 'Born at Tsat Sing Kong Village, Shap Pat Heung, Hong Kong; Cheung Lo Fat's Tomb; Born 14th September 1959; Died On 5th December 2007'.

Tang - W-2041 - this impressive black double, headstone was erected 'In loving memory of a devoted mother and grandmother and a loving father and grandfather. Tang Shih Gun 1937 – 1993 Tang Ng Siu Kwan 1929 - 2010', with the bottom of the headstone stating 'You will both be dearly missed'. The inscriptions on this headstone includes 'Erected By YangJu Sons & Grandsons. Grandma Deng Wushaoqun Born on 17 Nov 1937. Grandpa Deng Shu Geng Born on 12th June 1929. From Bao An City'.

George Po Man Wong - W-2037 - this headstone commemorates 'A loving Husband, Father, Brother and Uncle Born 15th December 1946 Died 2nd December 2011' with the base of the headstone stating 'Time Passes, Memories Stay, Loved And Remembered Every Day'. The headstone also states 'Wong Bao Wen's Tomb From HuiYang Town, Bao An city, GuangDong Province, China'. Wong was living at 18 Palmerston Road, Belfast when he died aged 64.

Wing Kan Tang - W-2040 - Tang is buried in the neighbouring plot to his parents mentioned above, with the headstone erected 'In memory of a dear husband and loving father Mr Wing Kan Tang Born on the

14th March 1970 Died on the 20th February 2015 You Will Never Walk Alone', with the base of the family headstone stating 'In him was life and the life was the light of men'. The inscriptions on this headstone includes 'Deng Yongqin 's Tomb. Born on 7th Feb Geng Xu [Geng Xu being the heavenly branch for the Year of the Dog 1970] Bao AN city. Died on 20 February YiWei [YiWei being the heavenly branch for the Year of Sheep 2015]'.

Ho Yuk Fong Chung - W-3082 - 'a dear sister, devoted friend and a loving mother Born on 26th November 1956 Died on Easter Sunday, 5th April 2015. Generous of heart, constant in faith, her deeds pure, her words kind, she gave willingly, never took'. The inscription on the headstone also records that this is Mother Zhong He Yufang's Tomb, and that she was born on 26 November BingSheng (BingSheng being the heavenly branch Year of the Monkey 1956) in Bao AN city, and died on 5 April YiWei (again YiWei being the Year of Sheep 2015).

Jonathan (Jonny) Li - Y-2934 - this headstone, which features a photo of a smiling Li, commemorates 'precious memories of Jonathan (Jonny) much loved son, devoted brother and grandson died 25th October 2016 age 24 years', with the base of the headstone reading 'You'll never walk alone'. A number of plaques adorn the grave including one to a 'special son always in our thoughts and forever in our hearts', another to a 'Special grandson. The happiness you brought in your own special way will be remembered always with love everyday'.

Wong Sang Tsang - Y-1762 - the wording in English on this headstone states 'In loving memory of Wong Sang. Beloved Husband And Father 21st June 1943 13th July 2018' with a photo of Tsang at the top of the headstone with the base stating 'Forever In Our Hearts'. The writing in Chinese to the left of the headstone states Hong Kong Sha Tau Kok where Tsang was born, with the wording to the right stating Tsang Wong Sang's Tomb and Beloved husband and father.

Trail 17 – Groups, Organisations and Workplaces

This trail is sponsored by my favourite organisation, EastSide Partnership, and I am indebted to the team, especially Chris Armstrong who has written the foreword to this publication, for their ongoing support.

This trail focuses on headstones where the dedications give a clue to the interred person's work or interests, and includes a number of references to Harland & Wolff, and the emergency services.

Alexander O'Neill - U-937 - hailing from a musical family, as a young man in the late 1940s and early 1950s, O'Neill played rhythm guitar in The Northern Troubadours, a band specialising in Hawaiian music. It was a family band, as his father Alexander senior played steel guitar, brother Stanley lead guitar with sister Muriel on vocals. During this time Ruby Murray was often performing on the same circuit, and Alexander's mother, Margaret, would sometimes help Murray with her stage makeup. Alexander O'Neill was the great-granda of EastSide Partnership's Lisa Rea Currie, with Lisa recalling that The Northern Troubadours were playing at Larne Town Hall on the day that the Princess Victoria sank. Alexander senior died on 25 September 1969 aged 69 whilst registered as living at 27 Belmont Street, Belfast, with his wife Margaret living at 78a Drumadoon Drive, Ballybeen when she died on 28 December 1986 aged 85. A guitar and musical notes with the words 'My God How Great Thou Art' below them feature on the

headstone, with Lisa's granda Alexander junior (Alex) commemorated as 'called home 5th May 2018' aged 84 whilst living at 7 Carwood Way, Glengormley.

Thomas J Gibbons - T-1792 - the logo of the Belfast Fire Brigade is at the top of this headstone commemorating 'Station Officer Thomas a beloved husband and father died 22nd June 1972' aged 57, whilst living at 50 Wheatfield Crescent, Belfast. Also buried in this grave is 'his dear wife Isabella a devoted mother and grandmother died 14th April 2003' aged 86 whilst also living at 50 Wheatfield Crescent. Also commemorated on this headstone is 'their grandson Fusilier Darren Hamilton Royal Welch Fusiliers [who] died 24th February 1992 aged 22 years'.

Robert (Bob) Alexander Wallace - S-1329 - 'a much loved brother and uncle, 6 January 1904 - 10 April 1975', Wallace was living at 9 Redcliffe Parade, Belfast when he died. This headstone also remembers 'Annie D. Miller nee Wallace beloved Mum of Elsie and Roy, also loving Granny and Great-Granny 17 June 1923 - 5 November 2017', and contains a Harland & Wolff logo and an image of a Singer sewing machine. The base of the headstone states 'Their absence is a silent grief, their life a beautiful memory'.

George Alexander Murdough - R-515 - a 'devoted husband', Murdough was living at 39 Emerald Street, Belfast when he died on 28 January 1985 aged 61. Also buried in this plot is 'his dear wife' Mary Edith Murdough who was living at 10 Toronto Street, Belfast when she died on 8 June 2008 aged 83. Along with a photo of the couple, the Northern Ireland Ambulance Service features prominently on this headstone.

Ernest Harris - R-2923 - Harris, 'a dear husband and father', was living at 66 Victoria Road, Sydenham, Belfast when he died on 14 November 1989 aged 51. The logo of the Maple Leaf Social & Rec Club features at the top of this headstone. The Maple Leaf Club was on Park Avenue, Belfast until a few years ago, and was originally a meeting spot for emigrants

heading to Canada on the first transatlantic flights from Belfast - hence the maple leaf in the name - in the days when you needed to be in a members club to get a visa. Passengers paid one pound each to join, but when the law changed and travel agents took over, the members got together and bought the club as an entertainment venue. Also buried in this plot is 'Eileen Loving mother, grandmother and great-grandmother died 3rd July 2012'.

George Convill - R-2683 - 'Born 21st May 1921 Died 11th February 1990' aged 68 whilst registered as living at 5 Iverna Street, Belfast. A RAOB (Royal Antediluvian Order of Buffaloes) logo is on this headstone below the words 'R.A.O.B. N.Ireland', with the words 'P.G.P. 1869' and 'No.4 Prov' either side of the logo. Also buried in this grave is 'Elizabeth Christina (Lily) [Convill] Born 7th May 1924 Died 14th August 2005' aged 81 whilst living at 86 Donegall Road, Belfast, 'Sadly missed by their children Olive, Chrissie, George, Gordon and grandchildren', with the base of this headstone reading 'together again'.

Fairhaven - R-3885 - a simple plaque at this plot states 'Fairhaven R. Jenkins W. Hewitt T. Neill'. Looking at the online burial records, it transpires that buried in this plot is Robert Jenkins who died on 22 October 1992 aged 83, William Hewitt who died on 19 April 1995 aged 87, and Thomas Neill who died on 28 October 1993 aged 93. Also buried in this plot, but not commemorated on the plaque is Samuel Kelso who died on 3 September 1996 aged 73. All four interments in this plot were living

at Fairhaven Nursing Home, 58 North Road, Belfast at the time of their deaths.

George Leslie Irwin - P-1352 - 'in loving memory of my dear son George Leslie died 1st November 1995' aged 47 whilst living at 13 Dover Court, Belfast. A plaque at the foot of this grave states 'will always be remembered by Officers and Members Shankill Road Campsie A.B.O.D.' (Apprentice Boys of Derry). Also buried in this plot is Margaret Ann Irwin who died on 12 July 1997 aged 89, whilst also registered as living at 13 Dover Court. Commemorated on this headstone is a 'dear husband Robert died 24th August 1969 interred at the City Cemetery' (grave 01-244 - Glenalina section) whilst living at 38 Mansfield Street, Belfast at the time of his death aged 61.

Daniel (Danny) McGreevy - P-3965 - McGreevy, 'a loving husband father and grandfather', was living at 28 Kilmuir Avenue, Dundonald when he died on 16 March 2000 aged 80, with his wife Mary, a 'much loved wife mum granny and greatgranny' dying at Dunlady Nursing Home, 18 Dunlady Road, Belfast on 3 February 2006 aged 81. This headstone contains logos for both Harland & Wolff and the Salvation Army.

Warnes - P-2325 - 'In loving memory of much-loved parents and grandparents Leslie died 2nd July 2000 [aged 82] and Maureen died 28th October 2000' aged 89, whilst both living at 16 Coolpark Avenue, Newtownbreda. This headstone contains an image of an anchor as well as the logo of the Joint Nursing & Midwives Council Northern Ireland, suggesting that Leslie was a sailor and that Maureen was perhaps a midwife.

Robert William Moore - P-2943 - ''Barney' died 26 April 2001 aged 38. Beloved father of Natasha Dedicated Volunteer of the Creative Arts Centre'. This headstone also contains a Manchester United club crest, with the bottom of the headstone stating 'always remembered'. At the base of the grave is a 'Best Dad' trophy and a heart-shaped plaque to a 'Special Dad. Miss you always. Love you forever'. Moore was living at 3 Sackville Court, Belfast at the time of his death, with the Creative Arts Centre located in Donegall Street, Belfast.

Daniel (Dan) O'Sullivan - P-2538 - 'passed away 14th May 2004' aged 91 whilst living at 10 Sussex Place, Belfast, having been predeceased by his wife Catherine (Tess) O'Sullivan who was living at 71 Vernon Street, Ormeau Road, Belfast when she 'passed away 11th May 1998' aged 83. This headstone contains the image of a budgie, as well as a train with the GNR (Great Northern Railway) logo, with the base of the headstone stating 'Think of us as you stand and pray Think of the family as it is today Stay together if you can Always remember Tess and Dan'.

Roland (Ron) Mills - P-3432 - 'a devoted husband, father and grandfather died 28th October 2004' aged 63, whilst registered as living at 9 Craigleith Drive, Dundonald. The Her Majesty's Prisons crest is at top of this headstone, with the base of this headstone stating 'You were the wind beneath my wings'. Mills appears to be the only interment in this plot.

Henry (Harry) Campbell - W-361 - this headstone commemorates 'a loving husband, father, grandfather and great-grandfather Born 17th August 1927 Called home 25th April 2006', and includes both the Harland & Wolff logo, and an image of both Samson and Goliath suggesting that Campbell was previously an 'island man'. Also commemorated on this headstone is 'his loving wife Emily beloved mother, grandmother and great-grandmother Born 19th May 1930 Called home 11th October 2019', with the headstone also featuring an image of the couple.

Thomas Henry (Harry) Miller - W-332 - 'a beloved husband, father and grandad Died 12th September 2006 aged 68 years' whilst living at 19 Lisnabreeny Road East, Belfast, with the base of the headstone stating 'Till we meet again'. The top of this headstone features the image of a pigeon, and the Comber Wildfowlers Association logo.

Raymond Cooke - W-718 - the top of this headstone features the Royal Navy Submarine Service's Dolphins badge below the words 'We Come Unseen'. One of the five fighting arms of the Royal Navy, the

Service is sometimes known as 'the Silent Service' as the submarines are generally required to operate undetected. Cooke was registered as living at 7 Old Mill Dale, Dundonald and is commemorated on the headstone as 'a loving husband [who] died 20th January 2007' aged 50.

John Bradshaw McFarlane - W-478 - 'treasured memories of my devoted partner one of nature's true gentlemen called home 30th May 2007' aged 75 whilst living at 13 Lawnview Street, Belfast. A photo of McFarlane wearing an Orange sash is on this headstone, as well as a logo with 'U.V.M & N.C. [Ulster Volunteer Medical and Nursing Corps] For God & Ulster' with four flags around the logo, and the words 'In God our trust' below the image of an open Bible. A plaque on the grave features an Orange sash, along with images of a star, bowler hat, umbrella and gloves.

Manus Mayes - W-1146 - Mayes (my Granny Craig's maiden name), 'a dearly loved father and partner', was living at 52 Leven Drive, Belfast when he died on 17 February 2008 aged 62. A photo of him, along with the Harland & Wolff logo, features on his headstone, with the base reading 'Peacefully sleeping, free from all pain, we wouldn't awake you to suffer again'.

George Calvert Brown - W-1382 - Brown, a 'loving husband, father and grandfather 10-7-1942 - 23-6-2011' was living at 18 Galway Park, Dundonald when he died aged 68. The logo of the Motor Racing Club of Ireland features on this headstone. Also buried in this grave is 'his loving wife June (nee Watson) Our beloved mother and grandmother 24-6-1945 - 29-4-2014 Together Again', along with the image of a daisy.

Veronica Tohill - W-2620 - the headstone, which contains the image of a cross and the logo of The Royal College of Nursing of the United Kingdom, was erected 'in loving memory of Veronica Tohill (nee Shannon) 19 May 1947 - 23 February 2014 Beloved wife and mother much loved grandmother. A Nurse who devoted her life to caring for others', with the base of her headstone stating 'Gave so much asked for so little'.

Thomas (Tommy) Wilson, MBE - T-216 - this headstone remembers a 'beloved son of Sarah & Edward died 30th May 2017' with images of RBP 813 and LOL 1892 either side of this inscription. Royal Black Preceptory 813 and Prince Albert Temperance LOL 1892 are both based in West Belfast. Also buried in this plot is Edward Wilson who was living at 135 Ebor Street, Belfast when he died on 30 August 1972 aged 72, Raymond Elliott who was living at 201 Tates Avenue, Belfast when he died on 23 November 1973 aged 33, and Sarah Wilson who was also living at 135 Ebor Street when he died on 18 May 1982 aged 70.

Trail 18 – Clergy

This trail is sponsored by Wesley Thompson, a former neighbour of mine in Dundonald many many moons ago and a fellow taphophile (a tombstone tourist).

This trail features 21 clergy from a number of denominations, and includes the extraordinary Rev Dr Roy Magee, O.B.E. My particular thanks to Robin Roddie for his help with this section, providing the detail on the Methodist Ministers featured in this section.

Rev. John Glass - D-635 - '1894 - 1956. Beloved husband of Muriel Florence Glass 1902-1985. Beloved parents of Rhoda Elizabeth Margaret Glass 1929-2017'. Rev. Glass was Irish President of Christian Endeavour at the time of his death, and was also a member of the Orange and Masonic Orders and a chaplain of the Royal Black Preceptory. Rev. Glass was living at the Methodist Manse, Moville, county Donegal, when he died on 23 October 1956 aged 62, with his wife living at 32 Broadacres, Templepatrick when she died on 22 January 1985 aged 82. Whilst there appears to be a recent appeal to rebuild the Methodist Church Hall in Moville, it seems that the only surviving active Methodist congregations on the Inishowen peninsula are at Glacknadrummond and Whitecastle.

Rev. Dr. Ernest Hamilton Williamson - D-651 - 'B.A PH.D,.Litt.B., 1892-1952. Minister of Ballyroney, Ballina and Tralee', in counties Armagh, Mayo and Kerry respectively. Rev. Williamson was living at 51 Knock Road, Belfast when he died on 6 May 1958 aged 66. Also buried in this plot is Rev Williamson's wife Hedwig Angelika Reichenbach Williamson, known as Heda, who was living at 27 Gilnahirk Avenue when she died on 25 February 1971, and Kevin Claude Williamson who died at Muckamore Abbey on 6 December 1989 aged 61.

Rev. William Logan Haslett - D-480 - 'Presbyterian Minister Castleblaney 1937 - 1952, Crumlin Road 1952 - 1960 Died 23rd February

1960' aged 50 whilst living at 87 Cliftonville Road, Belfast. Also commemorated on this headstone is 'his dearly loved wife Irene [who died] 4 December 1994' aged 84 whilst living at 12 Sandhurst Drive, Belfast, with the base of the headstone stating 'At Rest'.

Rev. Jim Patterson - D-754 - this headstone was erected 'in loving memory of Annie Wilhelmina Patterson dearly loved wife of Jim Patterson Senior Minister of Conlig Presbyterian Church died 14th June 1963' aged 80 whilst living at 34 Ardenlee Parade, Belfast and was buried on 17 June 1953. Rev. Patterson died on 11 May 1967 aged 94 whilst living at 26 Downshire Road, Bangor, with the couple's daughter Elizabeth Joan Patterson living at 48 Skipperstone Avenue, Bangor when she died on 15 June 1963 aged 63, and was buried on 17 June 1983, 20 years to the day after her mother's committal.

Robert Ferguson - D-2043 - 'Methodist Minister died 5th July 1964' aged 57, when his home address was recorded as the Methodist Manse, Cookstown. Rev. Ferguson's congregations included Lurgan from 1938-1942, Strabane 1942-1947, Dungannon 1947-1952, Agnes Street Belfast 1952-1957, before his final congregation in Cookstown from 1962. His obituary stated that 'he was frequently described as the possessor of the shepherd heart ... he did the work of an evangelist and used his rich gift of song in all his ministry.' Also buried in this grave is Rev. Ferguson's wife Emily Elizabeth Ferguson who died at Seapatrick Care Home, 80 Lurgan Road, Banbridge on 7 May 2003 aged 96.

Rev. Ivor Lawrence McCausland, B.Sc - D-2124 - 'died 18th November 1965 aged 24 years', whilst living at 48 Beechgrove Park, Belfast. 'Also his brother Michael Anthony McCausland died 13 July 1969 aged 22 years' whilst also living at 48 Beechgrove Park. So the McCausland brothers died within four years of each other, both before reaching their mid 20s. Also commemorated on this headstone is Margaret McCausland who was living at 190a Grand Parade, Belfast when she died on 12 January 1985 aged 64.

Rev. Thomas McMaster - U-52 - this headstone was erected 'in loving memory of Tom a very dear husband and father who passed through death into life 20th July 1966' aged 41, whilst registered as living at Trenola, Knockbreda Road, Belfast. Trenola is a large, detached house, now recorded as 7 Upper Knockbreda Road. Rev. McMaster was the minister of the nearby Glenburn Methodist Church at the time of his death. Rev. McMaster appears to be the only committal in this plot.

Rev. S. Gordon Young - U-670 - Rev. Young was living at 5 Maple Road, Clonskeagh, Dublin when he died on 31 January 1967 aged 60, with his headstone stating 'He walked with God'. Rev. Young was the minister of First Portadown Presbyterian Church, Edenderry from 1944-1947 before moving to Adelaide Road Presbyterian Church, Dublin. Also buried in this plot is 'his dear wife Ruth' who died at Gransha Hospital, Londonderry on 9 October 1989 aged 86.

Thomas Jackson - U-2282 - 'Methodist Minister' who died on 21 December 1968 age 67, with his wife Henrietta Jackson dying on 8 January 1977 aged 69, both whilst living at 9a Fortwilliam Drive, Belfast. Born in county Louth on 21 April 1901, Rev Jackson's congregations included Pettigo 1938-1943, Blacklion 1943-1948, Glastry and Portaferry 1951-1956, Richhill 1956-1961 and Ballynahinch 1961-1967. Rev. Jackson's obituary described him as 'an able expositor of the Word, his carefully prepared sermons reflected the width of his reading'. Also buried in this plot is the couple's son Arthur Jackson who was registered as living at 56 Drissold, Sutton Coldfield when he died on 28 December 1991 aged 53.

Rev. Andrew J C Leitch - T-3104 - Rev. Leitch, M.A., LL.B. was living at 4 Kincora Avenue, Belfast when he died on 1 May 1973 aged 59, with his wife Helen Douglas Leitch, L.R.A.M. living at 76 Marmont Park, Belfast when she died on 10 January 1985 aged 63. Licentiate of the Royal Academy of Music (LRAM) is a professional diploma, or licentiate, formerly open to both internal students of the Royal Academy of Music and to external candidates in voice, keyboard and orchestral instruments and guitar, as well as conducting and other musical disciplines.

Hugh Orr - U-737 - originally from Kilrea, county Londonderry, Rev. Orr was the minister of East End Baptist Church until 1958, when he was replaced as minister by Rev. Charles Lutton. In 1955 Rev. Orr conducted the wedding service of the parents of Russell Grant, sponsor of the RUC trail earlier in this publication, as per the photo below. This headstone was erected 'in loving memory of Pastor Hugh H. Orr died 10th November 1973', also commemorating 'his beloved wife Mary Eleanor died 19th July 1986'.

Rev. Henry Naisy Medd - C-845 - Rev. Medd is commemorated on this headstone as 'Died 9th February 1976', but he was not interred in this plot. Amongst Rev. Medd's congregations was Duncairn Gardens Methodist Church and, in 1952, he served as the President of the Methodist Church in Ireland. Buried in this grave is Rev. Medd's first wife Alice Elizabeth Medd who was living at 61 Onslow Parade, Belfast when she died on 9 August 1963 aged 81.

Frederick George Bell - C-348 - 'Senior Minister of Waterside Presbyterian Church and formerly Minister of Randalstown Old Congregation'. Reverend Bell was appointed to the ministry in Waterside Presbyterian Church in 1940 with Boys' Brigade company records showing that the date of company enrolment was 2 January

1941, when Rev. Bell was the chaplain. Randalstown Old Congregation Presbyterian Church is an oval-shaped church built in 1790, with the congregation dating back to 1655. It is possible that the oval design of the building is linked to that of St. Andrew's Church in Edinburgh which was built about six years earlier. Rev. Bell was living at 46 Deramore Drive, Belfast when he died on 8 March 1976 aged 81, with his wife Margaret Jane Bell living at 59 Bristow Park, Belfast when she died on 7 March 1978 aged 84.

Rev. Culbertson Jackson - C-360 - 'M.C.B. Sc. Died 5th October 1977. Dear husband, father and grandfather. A faithful servant of Jesus Christ', who was living at 42 Sicily Park, Belfast when he died aged 83. Rev. Jackson was minister of Crescent Presbyterian Church, University Road, Belfast for 32 years. Also buried in this grave is 'his beloved wife Mildred Isabella Jackson [who] died 4th April 1992' aged 88 at York House, Landsdowne Crescent, Portrush. The base of this headstone states "How many loved your moments of glad grace".

William John Hendren - S-3244 - Hendren died on '19th November 1980' and is recorded on this headstone as an 'Evangelist Church of Christ' aged 77 whilst registered as living at 418 Springfield Road, Belfast. Also buried in this plot is 'his beloved wife' Margaret Jane Hendren who died on 17 April 1988 aged 80, whilst living at 94 Joanmount Gardens, Belfast.

Rev. George Good - P-994 - 'A devoted husband, father and grandfather Born 6th October 1915 Died 31st May 1994' aged 78 whilst recorded as living at 30 Malone View Road, Belfast. Rev. Good was appointed to Greencastle Methodist Church in 1940 with the church flourishing until Easter 1941 when German bombs destroyed much of the area, with the Church itself sustaining serious damage. Rev. Good served in South Ceylon, Colombo from 1961-1965, and was then President of the Methodist Church in Ireland in 1969 whilst serving in Cork, before returning to Sri Lanka serving in Theololgical College of Lanka from 1971-1974, and was the supernumerary minister, i.e. retired minster, in Donegall Square Belfast (where he has also served from 1954-1958) from 1981 until his death. Also interred in this grave is his wife 'Eileen a loving wife, mother and grandmother and great-grandmother Born 3rd September 1922 Died 10th September 2014', with the base of the headstone stating '"For to me to live is Christ and to die is gain" Phil. 1 v. 21'.

Rev. Charles Logue B A - D-2321 - born in Londonderry on 17 March 1909, after study at Trinity College, Dublin and at Assembly's College, Belfast, Rev. Logue was licensed by the Presbytery of Derry on 15 May 1932 and ordained in Killala in June of the following year. In 1941 he moved to Fermoy and Lismore, where he remained for seven years, until he accepted a call to Kells and Ervey. After two years there he became minister of the congregations of 2nd Newtownhamilton and Creggan on 11 January 1950 and he remained in South Armagh for eleven and a half years. His final appointment was to Crossroads and Newtowncunningham, county Donegal where he served for thirteen years, retiring on 30 June 1974. Rev. Logue was living at 50 Clonallon Park, Belfast when he died on 13 December 2000 aged 91, whilst his 'beloved wife Janet 30th Dec 1911 - 19 Dec 2002' died at Strathearn Court Nursing Home, Belmont Road, Belfast, like her husband also aged 91 at the time of her death.

John Henry (Jack) Hodgins - P-2902 - commemorated on the headstone as '29th July 1921 - 19th March 2003 Clerk in Holy Orders in Christ Redeemed', Rev. Hodgins was living at 57 Sandhurst Drive, Belfast when he died aged 81. This headstone also commemorates 'his beloved wife Eunice Audrey 31st March 1922 - 29th August 2012 God giveth eternal life', with the couple 'Lovingly remembered by the whole family circle'.

Rev. Francois Murenzi - P-3368 - this headstone commemorates Rev. Murenzi '18. 2. 1963 – 19. 11. 2003 a loving husband devoted daddy and caring brother' who died, aged 40, whilst living at The Rectory, Church Road, Athy, county Kildare. The base of the headstone states 'Imana Ibarinde - God Bless You'.

Pastor John (Jack) Craig - P-3350 - this headstone commemorates 'a devoted husband died 7th February 2008' aged 82 whilst living in Bethany Lodge Nursing Home, 69 Osborne Park, Belfast. Craig was predeceased by his 'Beloved wife' Thelma Wilhelmina Craig who died at Orchard House Private Nursing Home, 2 Cherryvalley Park, Belfast on 2 August 2004 aged 80. The base of this headstone states 'Redeemed. At home with the Lord'.

Rev. Dr. Robert James (Roy) Magee, O.B.E - W-853 - 'a loving husband, father and grandfather died 31st January 2009 aged 79 years', Rev. Magee was living at 57 Old Dundonald Road, Dundonald at the time of his death. Ordained in the Presbyterian church in 1958 as minister at Sinclair Seamen's church in Belfast's docks area, in 1975 he moved to Dundonald where his reputation as an uncompromisingly fiery preacher and an effective mediator was consolidated. Rev. Magee then became actively involved with a cross-community alliance of clergymen and community workers. From 1990 Magee began protracted, private discussions with the Combined

Loyalist Military Command. Working in harness with Archbishop Robin Eames, the Church of Ireland primate, he set up indirect contacts with the British and Irish governments, a process which evolved into unprecedented undercover meetings between the Irish prime minister, Albert Reynolds, and loyalist leaders, and culminated in the 1994 cessation. Magee was predeceased by his son Royston (Roy) who died on 5 May 2005 aged 46, and his wife Maureen who died on 21 March 2007 aged 72.

Trail 19 – Titled

This trail is sponsored by Gavin Bamford, Chair of History Hub Ulster of which I am an associate member.

Trail 19 is entitled Titled and features a number of Sirs, MBEs and OBEs, including the legendary Tommy Patton.

Frederick Varty Spark CBE - D-356 - Spark was the Chief Accountant, Secretary and Director at Harland and Wolff when awarded the CBE in the New Years Honours of 1953, living at 39 Knockdene Park South, Belfast when he died on 12 August 1957 aged 72. Also buried in this grave is Norah Spark who died on 25 August 1962 aged 71, whilst registered as living at 64 Green Road, Knock, Belfast.

Sir William Frederick Neill - D-2291 - 'D.L., J.P., F.R.C.I.S., F.A.I. Lord Mayor of Belfast 1946-9, Member of Imperial Parliament 1945-50 died on voyage from South Africa and buried at sea 3rd January 1960. Erected by his loving wife Rhoda'. Born on 8 May 1889, Neill studied at Belfast Model School before becoming an estate agent. He was elected as an Ulster Unionist Party Alderman on the Belfast Corporation in 1938 and, as featured on this headstone, served as Lord Mayor of Belfast from 1946 to 1949. He was elected in the 1945 UK general election for North Belfast, serving five years, and was knighted in 1948. In 1954, he served as High Sheriff of Belfast, and then as Deputy Lord Mayor the following year. There appears to be no one presently buried in this plot, as Neill's wife Margaret (Rhoda) was buried in Belfast City Cemetery (J-455, City section) following her death on 19 January 1957, with a son 'Flight Sergeant W.F. Neill, killed at Dusseldorf 1943 aged 23 years' commemorated on a side panel.

Sir Richard Fredrick Roberts Dunbar, K.B.E, C.B. - C-2280 - 'died 17th October 1965' aged 65, whilst his wife 'Lady Ann Elizabeth Dunbar died 2nd October 1984', both whilst registered as living at 14 Knocklofty Park, Belfast. Head of the Northern Ireland Civil Service from 1961 until 1965, Sir Richard's portrait, painted in July 1964, hangs in the National Portrait Gallery. Also commemorated in this grave is 'their son Richard Robin Dunbar [who] died 19th January 2017'.

Sir John Harcourt - F-1 - '(Lord Mayor of Belfast) 1955-1957 Died 25th August 1969 aged 71 years'. A director of F. E. Harcourt and Company, coal merchants, Harcourt was High Sheriff of Belfast in 1949. After the death of John William Nixon, the independent Unionist MP for Belfast Woodvale (featured in my Dundonald Cemetery book), Harcourt stood

in the ensuing by-election on 4 April 1950 and was elected. In 1955, Harcourt was elected Lord Mayor of Belfast serving until 1957, when he was knighted. Harcourt was an active member of the Orange Order and a member of the Belfast lodge, Royal York LOL 145. Sir John's wife 'Lady Adelaide (Ada) Marie (nee Hopper) died 16th October 1965 aged 71 years', with both living at 60 Malone Road, Belfast when they died.

Alexander W Cussans O.B.E - T-3095 - Alexander William Cussans worked in Workman Clark before the Great War, then serving with 15th Battalion Royal Irish Rifles when he was wounded, before again returning to the front line. His brother and father also both served in Great War, with AW Cussans serving as the Chairman of the 15th Royal Irish Rifles O.C.A (Old Comorades Association). until his death. In 1951 Cussans was made an Ordinary Member of the Most Excellent Order of the British Empire (OBE) for service with the Ulster Special Constabulary, whilst registered as living at 121 Crumlin Road, Belfast. Cussans was living at Grahamsbridge Road, Dundonald when he died on 20 September 1972 aged 75, and was buried in Knockbreda Cemetery, before he was reinterred in Roselawn on 19 April 1973. Also buried in this grave is his wife Janie Cussans who died on 15 March 1975 aged 79, whilst also living at 1 Grahamsbridge Road.

Sir William McKinney - V-574 - 'Sir William McKinney C.B.E. LL.D. died 20th November 1979 aged 82 years', with his wife Lady Mary Ellen McKinney dying on 13 September 1980 aged 85, both whilst registered as living at 5 Deramore Park South, Belfast. Sir William was the owner of a laundry business and, along with Alistair McManus the head of a chain of shoe stores, had his home attacked by gunmen in February 1977 during a series of attacks on the business community. McManus survived a bullet wound to his neck, with Sir William escaping unhurt. Also buried in this plot is 'Robert Clyde McKinney 18th Oct. 1928 - 11th Oct. 2017' and 'Mary Elizabeth McKinney 17th Oct 1928 - 23rd Mar. 2018 (Robin and Betty)'.

Sir Arthur John Kelly - V-1387 - Kelly was made Commander of the Most Excellent Order of the British Empire (CBE) in 1950 when his details were listed as 'Cabinet Sercretariat, Stormont Castle attached to Home Office London', and was knighted in December 1960 when listed as 'Secretary to the Cabinet, Northern Ireland'. Sir Arthur was living at 6 Cherry Hill, Malone Road, Belfast when he died on 27 May 1983 aged 84. Also buried in this plot is his wife Lady Florence Mary Kelly who was living at 148 Malone Road, Belfast when she died on 8 April 1986 aged 87.

William A McKnight, MBE - D-454 - 'Teacher and musician. Beloved husband and father died 10 March 1984' aged 69. McKnight was awarded the MBE in 1968 when Principal of Strandtown Primary School, Belfast, and was living at 227 Kings Road, Belfast when he died. Also buried in this plot is Evelyn Violet (Vevey) McKnight née Small who died 13 June 1999 aged 75 whilst also living at 227 Kings Road, William James McClurg who died on 3 October 1957 aged 62, and Elizabeth F McClurg who died on 18 August 1974 aged 89 both whilst living at 54 Loopland Park, Belfast. 'Dr Susan M McKnight [who] died 3rd March 2012' is also buried in this plot with the base of the headstone stating 'O rest in the Lord'.

Thomas (Tommy) William Saunderson Patton OBE - T-350 - Patton worked at Harland and Wolff for 29 years from 1932, and was elected to Belfast City Council for the Ulster Unionist Party (UUP) at the 1973 local election. He retired in 1982, but continued to sit on the council, serving as Lord Mayor of Belfast that year. He was appointed High Sheriff of Belfast for 1992/3. Patton has been described by journalist Jim McDowell as an example of a 'cornerstone of what the unionist working class vote was'. Sinn Féin's Máirtín Ó Muilleoir noted Patton's malapropisms, giving, as an example, 'the police are no detergent against the IRA'. A park in East Belfast is named in his memory. Patton was living at 89 Park Avenue, Belfast when he died on 20 October 1993 aged 79, with his wife Alice living at the same address when she died on 25 June 1990 aged 68.

Sir James (Jim) Alex Kilfedder - C-1708 - born in Kinlough, county Leitrim to a family from Enniskillen, Kilfedder was educated at Portora Royal School, Enniskillen and Trinity College Dublin. During his time in college he acted as auditor of the College Historical Society, one of the oldest undergraduate debating societies in the world. He became a barrister, practising in London. On 20 March 1995, while travelling by train into London from Gatwick airport, Kilfedder died of a heart attack aged 66, whilst registered as living at 96 Seacliffe Road, Bangor. 20 March 1995 was the same day that the Belfast Telegraph carried a front-page story saying that an Ulster MP had been targeted as one of twenty MPs invited by the LGBT rights organisation OutRage! in a letter to come out. Kilfedder died unmarried, survived by two sisters, and was described as 'a phenomenon or perhaps a left-over from a remote era of Northern Irish politics'. James was predeceased by his father Robert who was living at 1 Knockburn Park, Belfast when he died on 7 August 1964 aged 88, and his mother Elizabeth who was living at Eastonville, Donaghadee Road, Millisle when she died on 6 February 1968 aged 76.

Mary Curlett, MBE - C-2377 - a school caretaker awarded the MBE in 1994, Curlett was living at 84 Alverston Park, Carryduff when she died on 23 January 1997 aged 62. Also buried in this plot is Anne Curlett who died on 13 June 1965 aged 56, and George Curlett who died on 21

August 1987 aged 76, both living at 18 Timbey Park, Belfast when they died.

Margretta (Gretta) Falloon MBE - P-3342 - this headstone commemorates a 'loving wife, inspirational mum and loyal friend'. Falloon was a social worker described as 'a rough no-nonsense type' working on the Braniel Estate, with her death notice stating: 'Death leaves a heartache no-one can heal, love leaves a memory no-one can steal. Deeply missed by loving husband Tommy, daughter Margaret, son Trevor and daughter-in-law Elaine'. Gretta was living at 22 Braeside Grove, Braniel when she died on 24 October 2004 aged 59.

Margaret Elizabeth (Peggy) Hoey, MBE - D-1115 - 'died 5th February 2010 a loving wife, mother and Granny'. Hoey was awarded the MBE in 1996 whilst recorded as a 'Typist, Lord Chancellor's Department', living at 17 Glencairn Street, Belfast when she died aged 73. Also buried in this plot is Hoey's father David McAlpine who died on 6 March 1960 aged 57, and her mother Vina Maude McAlpine who died on 13 November 1977 aged 77, both whilst also living at 17 Glencairn Street.

Professor Sir Bernard Crossland - W-1472 - born in London on 20 October 1923, Crossland entered employment as an engineering apprentice with Rolls-Royce, gaining his education through part-time study, culminating in the award of a PhD from the University of Bristol in 1953. His teaching career began at Luton Technical College in 1945, before he became Professor of Mechanical Engineering at The Queen's University of Belfast, where he went on to act as Pro-Vice Chancellor. Elected as a Fellow of the Royal Society in 1979, Crossland was appointed Commander of the Order of the British Empire in 1980,

and a Freeman of the City of London in 1987. After retirement he became involved in the investigation of several accidents, the most noteworthy of which was the King's Cross Fire. He then served as an Emeritus Professor of Chemical Engineering at Queen's University of Belfast, and was knighted in 1990. Sir Bernard died on 17 January 2011 aged 87, whilst living at 16 Malone Court, Belfast.

Sir George Quigley CB, PhD - W-2530 - commemorated on this headstone as 'A beloved husband 26 November 1929 - 3 March 2013' aged 83, Sir George Quigley held several high-profile positions in the Civil Service before embarking on a successful career in the private sector. In 1988, he joined the Ulster Bank and became its chairman. He was also a director of the Belfast aerospace company, Short Brothers. Sir George was one of two independent witnesses who verified the decommissioning of weapons by the loyalist paramilitary group, the Ulster Defence Association (UDA). He also headed an industrial taskforce seeking a reduction in corporation tax, and was the author of a government report that called for the Northern Ireland Parades Commission to be scrapped and reconstituted. Sir George passed away after becoming ill during morning worship at Helen's Bay Presbyterian Church, with the base of his headstone reading 'The Lord's My Shepherd'.

Gordon Burnison, OBE - W-2622 - 'beloved husband and father 8th February 1930 - 11th March 2014'. Burnison received the OBE in the New Years Honours of 1990 when he was the Director of the Federation of Building and Civil Engineering Contractors. On 1 June 1944, a United States Army Air Force B-17 Flying Fortress came down on Cavehill, Belfast, killing all 10 crew members on board, and 14-year old Burnison witnessed the crash. Interviewed in *The News Letter* on 2

June 2006, Burnison stated 'That morning I forgot about school and ran up to Cavehill to see what happened. The plane was in among the trees. The ammunition was exploding in the heat. The Fire Brigade arrived and brought the bodies out on stretchers covered in blankets'.

Alessie McCrossan, MBE - P-2283 - a 'beloved sister and our much loved aunt called home 8th September 2016'. Miss McCrossan received the MBE in 2001 'for services to the community', whilst the Alessie Centre on the Shankill Road - which houses the greater Shankill Early Years Project and offers working or studying parents a child-minding service and drop-in centre - is named after her. This headstone also commemorates 'a beloved sister and aunt Mary (Maisie) called home 8th April 1999 aged 79' whilst living at 29 Florence Square, Belfast, and 'our beloved brother Bobby called home 15th January 2003' aged 74 whilst living at Clifton House Nursing Home.

Bridget Nesbitt, MBE - W-2917 - 'Beloved Wife, Mother and Grandmother Died 3rd February 2018 Aged 82'. Also remembered on this headstone is Bridget's husband 'Bryan Nesbitt A Beloved Husband, Father and Grandfather Died 15th April 2015 Aged 78'. The headstone features an RAF logo, and an image of the couple.

Hugh Sterrett, MBE - V-2209 - 'a loving husband, devoted father and grandfather called home 15th April 2019', Sterrett was the senior attendant at Knockbreda Cemetery, and was awarded the MBE in April 2005 for services to local government. Sterrett's funeral notice stated that he was 'late of Ballysillan Road, beloved husband of Sally, much loved father of Pauline and partner Mark, devoted grandfather of Brenda, Gareth and great grandchildren Marcus and Mason' with his funeral service held in Ballysillan Elim Church. From conversations

with Council staff at Knockbreda Cemetery in the course of compiling my *2020* book, it is clear that Hugh certainly deserved his award, acknowledging many years' service in the cemetery. Hugh had initially wanted to work as a butcher and came to Knockbreda to work for a few weeks with his father. Hugh worked at Knockbreda Cemetery for a total of 59 years, succeeding his father in the role.

Dr Ian Adamson O.B.E - Y-2265 - this striking headstone with the representation of a tree at the top, commemorates 'Dr. Ian Adamson O.B.E. 1944 - 2019 Mitakuye Oyasin', a phrase from the Lakota people of North America meaning 'All Are Related'. Born in Bangor on 28 June 1944. Adamson was raised in Conlig, becoming a specialist in Community Child Health (Community Paediatrics). An Ulster Unionist member of Belfast City Council from 1989, he served as Deputy Lord Mayor in 1994-95 and then Lord Mayor of Belfast in 1996–97 and was awarded the OBE in 1998 for services to local government. My favourite story of Dr Adamson is from his time as Lord Mayor. His skill as a gifted linguist, as evidenced by his headstone, was proven when a group of Sioux Indians visited Belfast City Hall and, to their amazement, Adamson greeted them in their native tongue. Adamson was an MLA for Belfast East from 1998 until 2003, and was involved in many other projects including the establishment of the Somme Heritage Centre, now Museum, at Conlig in 1994, Adamson also served as a member of the Ulster-Scots Agency, and was President of the Belfast Civic Trust. Adamson, who described himself as "a British Unionist, an Irish Royalist and an Ulster Loyalist", died on 9 January 2019 aged 74.

Margaret (Meg) Holmes MBE - U-1852 - 'Devoted to all her family and a dedicated servant to her community died 7th July 2019 aged 88'. Holmes's main death notice stated 'late of 13 Cliftondene Crescent. Dearly beloved wife of the late James Holmes and loving mother and mother-in-law to son Terry and Tanya, son Stephen and Belle and daughter Janice, devoted grandmother and great grandmother'. Also buried in this plot is her 'dear husband and father James J Holmes died 17th April 1968' aged 49 whilst also living at 13 Cliftondene Crescent, Belfast.

Trail 20 – And Finally

This last trail is also sponsored by John Costley to whom I am grateful for his ongoing support.

This final trail contains nice sentiments written on headstones (not that people are going to write critical sentiments).

Mona Lagard Algeo - U-482 - 'Born 22nd Sept 1901 Died 6th July 1966' living at 35 Downshire Park Central, Bangor when she died. Also buried in this plot is 'Thomas Henry Algeo Born 25th November Died 25th April 1968' who was living at 66 Grange Crescent, Bangor when he died on 25 April 1968 aged 67. The base of this headstone states 'death is just a door set gently ajar for weary feet that have travelled afar nothing to dread or fear at all only safe sheltering as shadows fall'.

John Burrows - T-1434 - 'in loving memory of my dearly beloved husband John died 14th May 1971' aged 65 whilst registered as living at 44 Cabin Hill Gardens, Belfast. 'When a good man dies. For years beyond our ken, The light he leaves behind Shines on the paths of men'. Also buried in this plot, but not commemorated on the headstone, is Caroline Burrows who died on 23 April 1985 aged 79, whilst also living at 44 Cabin Hill Gardens.

Robinson - T-1535 - commemorated on this headstone below a photo of North Belfast with Cavehill in the background is 'a loving husband and father John 25th May 1909 - 25th October 1971 aged 62 and 'Mary Ann May [Robinson] nee Kelly 21st April 1923 - 30th October 2008' aged 85. 'An empty room with vacant chair, the deafening roar of silence. Our Love, Memories and Faith in Christ shall endure forever'. Also commemorated on this headstone is 'their much loved only son Gerald Frederick Gerry 30th June 1953 - 2nd January 2011 [aged 57]. End of the Robinson line. In God's Hands'. All three were living at 39 Slievecoole Park, Belfast at the time of their deaths.

Noelle Parker - T-30 - 'born in Enniskillen 22nd Dec. 1937 died in New York City 9th Oct 1971'. Parker's address at the time of her death was 41/15/40 Fourth Long Island and she was buried on 15 October 1971. The verse of this headstone describes Parker as 'A thoughtful mind, a beautiful soul, the loveliest girl, I'll ever know. I love you always'.

Butler - V-59 - this headstone commemorates 'Rachel Butler 1915 - 1972' and 'David Butler 1910 - 1980' who lived at 150 Cambrai Street, Belfast when they died. A plaque on the headstone from their children Iris, David, Brian and Wilson, along with a photo of the smiling couple, states, 'We thank you for giving us life, we thank you for giving us our childhood, we thank you for giving us a happy family environment. We thank you for teaching us right from wrong; and we thank you for giving us all your love, but most of all we thank God for giving us: David & Rachel Butler as our parents. We will always remember both of you. God bless'.

William Gilmour - T-1790 - this headstone commemorates 'William (Billy) a dear husband and devoted father [who] died 11th June 1972' aged 40 whilst living at 41 Clara Park, Belfast. Also buried in this plot is Billy's daughter 'Edna Gillen [a] much loved wife and mother died 14th September 2017', with the headstone then stating 'Cherish life. Tomorrow is promised to no one'. The words 'Mizpah' (Hebrew for 'watchtower', as mentioned in the Bible story of Jacob and Laban, making a pile of stones marked an agreement between two people, with God as their watching witness) and 'Gen[esis] 15. 31-49' are at the foot of the headstone.

Thomas Elliott - T-4111 - Thomas died on 6 January 1975 aged 73, with his wife Lily dying on 5 December 1975 aged 65, both whilst living at 8 Windsor Road, Belfast. The base of the headstone states: 'I said to the man who stood at the gate of the year "Give me a light that I may tread safely into the unknown" and he replied - "Go out into the darkness and put your hand into the hand of God. That shall be to you better than light and safer than a known way'.

Dave Adair - S-1352 - this headstone records 'Cherished memories of a beloved husband and father died 16th March 1975' aged 42 whilst living at 25 Abbeydale Parade, Belfast. The base of the headstone states: 'No late light has lightened up my heaven, no second morn has ever shone for me, all my life is bliss from thy dear life was given, all my life is bliss as in the grave with thee. Mizpah'.

Andrew Cairns - R-1030 - 'High Sheriff of Belfast died 20th March 1985' aged 72. Cairns was living at 21 Lisburn Avenue, Belfast at the time of his death, and he appears to have died in Office. A plaque at the bottom of his headstone to 'Granda my guardian angel' states 'I love you with all my heart, and know that you love me with all of yours. I was truly blessed to have you for my Granda, and heartbroken when you had to leave. Look after my heart for you have that broken peace [sic] with you. Always and forever Andrea xx'.

Andrews - S-1835 - 'In loving memory of our dear Dad and Mum' Samuel Andrews who died on 19 July 1977 aged 72, with Margaret Andrews dying on 20 May 1982 aged 69, whilst both living at 25 Shankill Parade, Belfast. Also commemorated on this headstone is 'Our dear niece Caroline Rose [Andrews] died 29th June 1985' aged 18 whilst living at 31 Wheatfield Drive, Belfast and she is remembered with the following tribute on this headstone: 'We often lie awake at night when others are asleep. We walk alone down memory lane, as the tears roll down our cheeks. No one knows the heartache we try so hard to hide. Some people say as time goes by, the heartache will subside. The feelings in our hearts today, are the same the day you died, but now you're with Our Lord in heaven, and by his right hand side. It broke our hearts to lose you, your parting caused such pain, but the greatest day has yet to come when we will meet again'.

Kathleen Thompson - V-2657 - this headstome commemorates 'Our dear mother Kathleen Died 17th August 1991' aged 53 whilst living at 262 Ormeau Road, Belfast, whilst also buried in this grave is Valerie Shaw 'died 19th November 2002' aged 56 whilst living at 20 Somerset Street, Ormeau Road, Belfast. The base of the headstone reads 'Your great sense of humour will see me through. It was sheer magic love'.

Ronald Ernest Lee, M.B.E - F-86 - Lee was living 1 Prince Edward Drive, Belfast when he died on 23 December 1992 aged 63. Below Lee's details on the headstone is "Faire Is The Heaven". Faire Is The Heaven, by William Harris, starts: Faire is the heav'n, where happy souls have place, In full enjoyment of felicitie, Whence they doe still behold the glorious face, Of the divine, eternal Majestie. Also buried in this grave is Lee's father James Lee who was living at 19 Ridgeway Street, Belfast when he died on 4 November 1965 aged 63, and his mother Letitia Lee who was living at Haypark Residential Home, Belfast when she died on 30 June 1992 aged 92.

Edward Duncan - P-1363 - 'died 18th January 1996, aged 33. A loving husband and Daddy. Yes we were special, Memories I treasure of being together, are in my heart 'always and forever''. Also commemorated on this headstone is 'Our baby daughter Rachael Victoria died 29 January 1996, aged 15 days. Precious were our days together, In my heart these I treasure, Night night wee honey'. Edward appears to have died four days after his daughter was born, with his daughter then dying 11 days later, with both recorded as living at 32 Fourwinds Park, Belfast at the time of their deaths, and images of both of this headstone.

Susan Jayne Wilson - W-799 - this headstone was erected 'in loving memory of Susan Jayne My Beloved Wife 22nd November 1949 22nd August 2007' aged 57, whilst living at 1 Millars Close, Dundonald. As well as the image of

Wilson, the headstone contains what seems to have been a letter to her family penned by her: 'Goodbye my family, my life is past. I loved you to the very last. Weep not for me but courage take, Love each other for my sake. For those you love don't go away. They walk beside you every day'.

Joy - W-1896 - this headstone remembers 'Robert Charles (Rab) loving husband caring dad and mischievous Granda Born 11/04/1928 - Died 20/10/2009' and 'Henrietta (Hedy) Loving wife, caring mum, storyteller, granny Born 17/05/1931 - Died 25/11/2017', and contains an image of the couple, as well as a person sheltering under an umbrella and a Holy Bible with the name 'Nora Roberts' on the front cover. A plaque at the foot of the grave remembers 'My darling husband Rab much loved Dad, Granda, Paps Da, Charlie, Rab a Dab. Forever in our hearts Isaiah 49:15-16' and 'my darling wife Hedy much loved Mum, Gran Blossom Queen of Sheba Henny McCoubrey Forever in our hearts'.

Trevor Ferguson - S-4228 - '"Forever young" Our precious Trevor Ferguson (Wee Trev) found everlasting peace 18th July 2010 aged 25 years'. A plaque on the grave with a photo of Ferguson states '30/10/1984 18/07/2010. I miss the funny looks, I miss the laughter, I miss the craic, but most of all I miss you'. Also buried in this plot is William Dunseith who died on 14 May 1984 aged 59, and Mabel Dunseith who died on 30 April 1997 aged 76, all living at 39 Boundary Street, Belfast.

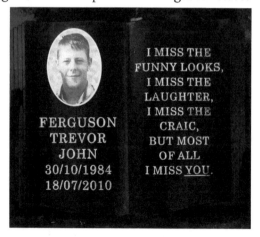

Kirkpatrick - T-124 - the long text on this headstone reads 'My life is but a weaving Between my Lord and me, I cannot choose the colours

He worketh steadily. Oftimes He weaveth sorrow, And I in foolish pride, Forget He sees the upper And I, the underside. Not till, the loom is silent And the shuttles cease to fly Shall God unroll the canvas And explain the reason why. The dark threads are as needful In the Weaver's skillful [sic] hand As the threads of gold and silver In the pattern He has planned'. Interred in this grave is Elizabeth (Lily) Kirkpatrick who died on 13 November 1972 aged 75, and William Kirkpatrick who died on 21 April 1973 aged 73, both whilst living at 85 Ballygomartin Road, Belfast, Mary Elizabeth (May) Campbell who died at Abingdon Manor, 949 Crumlin Road, Belfast on 26 January 2002 aged 80, and 'Grandson and Son Pastor Alan J. Campbell died 12th June 2017'.

June Day - R-1857 - a plaque at this grave, accompanied by a photograph of Day, commemorates 'A loving wife, mother, daughter and sister 30th June 1950 to 26th October 2005. An Irish blessing. May the road rise up to meet you, May the wind be always at your back, May the sun shine warm upon your fields and until we meet again, May God you in the palm of His hand'. Interred in this grave is Day's mother Margaret Mahood who died on 13 November 1987 aged 60, and her father John Mahood who died on 9 September 2003 aged 76, both whilst living at 124 Malton Drive, Belfast.

Anne Victoria Dugan - R-1803 - 'precious memories of my loving wife Anne Victoria a devoted mother and grandmother called home 11th June 2012', with the base of the headstone stating 'Keep her Jesus in Thy keeping, until I reach that golden shore, then dear saviour let me have her, and love her as I did before'. This plot also contains the remains of Victoria McConnell who died on 22 June 1987 aged 71, and

William McConnell who died on 18 February 1988 aged 76, both whilst living at 88 Greystown Avenue, Belfast.

Graeme Hutchinson - Y-1629 - this headstone commemorates 'Graeme (1970 - 2018) So Special!' with the word 'SPECIAL' vertically on the headstone, accompanied by the following; 'Scriptures his delight Precious husband & best friend Enjoyable company Courageous in illness Inspirational in life Altogether amazing man Loved, so much loved!'. The bottom of the headstone reads 'Rejoicing in Christ's Presence today', with the base of the headstone reading 'In the house of the Lord forever'.

Tom Anderson - Y-2358 - this headstone recalls 'Treasured memories of Tom much loved husband, father and grandfather 18-4-1951 - 30-4-2021', with an inscription at the base of the headstone stating 'Beidh Muid Le Cheile Mo Chroi', Irish for 'we will be together my love'. Plaques on the grave also state 'They say time heals all sorrow and helps us to forget, but time has only proven how much we miss you yet', and 'In loving memory [of] someone special. Blessed with a wonderful nature and a loving caring way. You left many happy memories to treasure every day'.

Photo Credits

Page 23 – Karen Blaney
Page 27 – Billy Hunter
Page 32 – Russell Grant
Page 43 – John Costley
Page 47 – Julie Roulston
Page 54 – David Francis
Page 66 – Nigel Henderson
Page 69 – Alistair McCartney
Page 75 – Leslie Anderson
Page 93 – Belfast Telegraph
Page 98 – Belfast Telegraph
Page 110 – Elizabeth & Ivan Towe
Page 115 – Stewart McCracken
Page 131 – Lisa Rea Currie
Page 141 – Russell Grant

L - #0292 - 240122 - C0 - 210/148/9 - PB - DID3253757